Studies in Shakespeare

AMS PRESS
NEW YORK

UNIVERSITY OF MIAMI PUBLICATIONS

IN

ENGLISH AND AMERICAN LITERATURE

VOLUME I   MARCH, 1953

Studies
in Shakespeare

EDITED BY

ARTHUR D. MATTHEWS

and CLARK M. EMERY

UNIVERSITY OF MIAMI PRESS

CORAL GABLES, FLORIDA

1953

Copyright © 1953, by the University of Miami
Reprinted from the edition of 1953, Coral Gables
First AMS EDITION published 1971
Manufactured in the United States of America

International Standard Book Number: 0-404-04267-8

Library of Congress Number: 79-144658

AMS PRESS INC.
NEW YORK, N.Y. 10003

THE DEPARTMENT OF ENGLISH of the University of Miami inscribes this volume of Shakespearean studies by various distinguished scholars to Professor William L. Halstead, long-time Chairman of the Department, under whose direction the University of Miami's Shakespeare Conference was originated in 1951.

In this dedication I gladly concur, recommending the volume to other scholars as worthy of their notice and as the first of a series of studies in English and American literature to be published under the imprint of the University of Miami Press.

B. F. Ashe
President
University of Miami

October, 1952

Preface

In 1951 the University of Miami initiated a Shakespeare conference which was held in conjunction with
the University's Shakespeare Festival. In the following
year the Conference was to such a degree expanded that
publication of the papers there delivered appeared
desirable. This volume contains twelve of the fourteen
papers. "Is There a Case for Goneril and Regan?"
by Paul Parnell (New York University) was unavailable
for publication; as co-editor of this volume, Clark
Emery withdrew his *The Extasie* Reconsidered."

A. D. M.
C. M. E.

Contents

A Definitive Text of Shakespeare:
Problems and Methods

by FREDSON BOWERS

IN THE EARLY NINETEENTH CENTURY the great Shakespearian editor, Edmund Malone, wrote as follows: "Though to explain and illustrate the writings of our poet is a principal duty of his editor, to ascertain his genuine text, to fix what is to be explained, is his first and immediate object; and till it be established which of the ancient copies is entitled to preference, we have no criterion by which the text can be ascertained."[1] For its time this was a remarkably advanced statement, even though it is cast in general terms, and is in part incomplete. It stands as an effective protest against the unprincipled eclecticism of most eighteenth-century editors, but it would scarcely be accepted today as an adequate summary of editorial position except in the very simplest of cases where an editor's investigation discloses that there is only a single text which has any claim whatever to authority.

We may contrast this with the latest scientific principle formulated by Sir Walter Greg in his "Rationale of Copy-Text"[2] and strikingly illustrated in his recent edition of Ben Jonson's *Gipsies Metamorphosed*.[3] According to Greg, the editor's first duty is to establish the genetic relationship of all early texts in order to determine which one stands closest to an author's autograph papers. That edition is to have general authority as regards the forms of the accidentals; that is, the framework of spelling, punctuation, and capitalization in which the substantives, or meaningful words, are cast. If all other editions are simple reprints, this selected early text—which the editor under any circumstances must choose as his copy-text—also becomes the only text of authority for the substantives; and any alteration of its wording must be viewed as emendation. On the other hand, if some different early edition has received an infusion of fresh authority and in various of its substantives may be taken as representing some other transcriptional link back to the author or his papers, substantive authority may be divided. One text may, in general, be 'preferred' (to use Malone's language) as purer in its texture of accidentals and very likely in some considerable number of indifferent verbal readings; the other text may, also in general, be 'preferred' for various purer readings or specific authorial revisions in the substantives.

---

1 Boswell's *Malone's Shakespeare* (1821), I, 202-203.
2 *Studies in Bibliography*, III (1950), 19-36.
3 Oxford University Press, for The British Academy (1952).

It is clear that in complex cases we can no longer theorize in such vague terms as of establishing a single early edition which can be preferred in every respect to all other texts and which can be set up as a criterion. Authority may be divided, and in a few of the more intricate textual problems in Shakespeare this authority may even shift back and forth between early editions of the same play both as to accidentals and to substantives.[4]

Until the twentieth century it is in general true that no scientific methods had been evolved for determining the divided authority of early texts, principally because the methods had not been invented for arriving at any just concept of the nature and history of the manuscripts which served as printers' copy for Shakespeare's plays. Hence the definition of what constitutes a 'preferred' or authoritative text perforce remained hazy save for those plays first printed in the Folio. Long before the Globe edition, simple Folio reprints had been separated from their quarto copy, and general preference established for the earlier quarto text; but specific preference in the choice of individual readings was still made—by and large—by no other criterion than the editors' literary taste. Moreover, if I am right in my assumption that Malone's statement was chiefly aimed at the problem of emendation,[5] even well into the present century little progress had been made from his general position. Editors, of course, followed the Malone precept and ceased to base a text on a late quarto or a Folio reprint; but in all cases where more than one early edition seemed to claim independent authority, the methods had not been evolved to determine the validity of the respective claims and, equally important, to define their extent.[6]

The textual revolution instigated and guided chiefly by Pollard, Greg, and McKerrow[7] provided these methods and vastly cleared the air by the introduction of bibliographical principles. Yet we must recognize that there are at present available only a few Shakespearian texts which have utilized

[4] If it could be positively demonstrated that the early part of Q2 *Hamlet* was printed directly from an annotated copy of the 'bad quarto' Q1, and not from manuscript with occasional reference to Q1 when difficulties arose (as seems more likely), F1 would provide the only transcriptional link with a Shakespearian manuscript for these scenes, except for the Q2 substantive variants from Q1 and the Q2 lines wanting in F1. The generally accepted hypothesis that Q2 was set from Shakespeare's 'foul papers' would enforce the selection of Q2 as copy-text for all lines set from this manuscript. But if the memorially reconstructed Q1 served as physical copy for the early scenes, logic would compel selection of F1 for these scenes in order to secure accidentals that have some direct transcriptional link with a Shakespearian manuscript. This would hold even if an editor preferred in general to follow the substantive readings of Q2 rather than of F1 for this section. I do not recall having seen this point raised previously for *Hamlet*, doubtless since the precise details of the Q1 - Q2 relationship are still very much in question.

[5] Unless the statement is to be taken as completely circular, this is the way I suspect we must interpret "and till it be established which of the ancient copies is entitled to preference, we have no criterion by which the text can be ascertained." The text is seemingly not ascertained by establishing the preferred copy; instead, only a criterion is secured on which to base the ascertainment of the text, presumably by emendation in case of supposed error.

[6] However, one must not overlook the pioneer work of P. A. Daniel in this respect and of one or two Continental scholars.

the methods of this revolutionary approach, though many years have since elapsed.

Our present position, therefore, is this. Although the tools for reform have been in our hands for many years, we are still reading, and quoting, and criticizing from a standard Shakespeare text evolved over eighty years ago for the Globe edition, long before modern standards of textual criticism were formulated.[8] It is as though we had in the garage a modern streamlined hundred and fifty horsepower automobile, but when we took it out we found we could jolt only in second gear over the rutted back-country roads of the horseless carriage era. What we must have is a new standard text to displace the Globe and its Old Cambridge derivative. For various reasons too complex to explore here, I believe this new definitive text must be an old-spelling one if it is to fulfill the needs of present-day scholarship for a text which will serve as a norm for reading, study, and reference,[9] and as a new foundation on which popular modernized reading texts can be constructed. I must ask you also to assume with me that it must not be a mere diplomatic reprint of some single authority, like the Variorum, but instead a critically edited and therefore an eclectic text which, making use of the most advanced bibliographical, critical, and linguistic techniques, will achieve the maximum recovery of what Shakespeare wrote in every possible detail, no matter how minute.

Such an old-spelling text was begun by the late R. B. McKerrow. But only its *Prolegomena* was published,[10] and since that date, 1939, the work has not been carried forward, no text for any play in the series has appeared, and none is likely to be brought out in the near future.[11] In truth, the enormous difficulties in the project have undoubtedly appalled prospective candidates, for the work that still needs to be done to provide the proper basis for such an edition is enough to make the boldest editor pause. It is clear that this new definitive edition must be freshly constructed from the ground up. It cannot be simply a revision and refinement of some

---

7 On a different level one might add Dover Wilson, who has often attempted to be bibliographical although his grasp of the method and its discipline has not been secure, and his identification with the so-called 'bibliographical school' has done it more harm than good. McKerrow specifically excepted the Wilson conjectural method from bibliography; see also Hereward Price. "Towards a Scientific Method of Textual Criticism in Elizabethan Drama," *JEGP*, XXXVI (1937), 151 - 167, although he mistakenly accepts the Wilson techniques as bibliographical.

8 In spite of some real virtues the New Cambridge edition has failed to provide a new standard text, in part through critical distrust of some of its more speculative elements and in part, perhaps, because of certain eccentricities in the details of its presentation.

9 To illustrate a typical problem in modern scholarship: a few years ago a friend had occasion to quote some lines from the early section of *Hamlet* and asked my advice about the best text. After we had canvassed the problems, in despair he went back to the Globe lines, as at least traditional.

10 *Prolegomena for the Oxford Shakespeare: A Study in Editorial Method* (Oxford, 1939).

11 Information privately communicated now indicates that the Clarendon Press has at last selected a new editor and that the McKerrow edition will be carried forward to completion by the brilliant young textual critic, G. I. Duthie. This is very good news indeed.

already existing text, as almost all complete Shakespeare editions have been since the Globe. Moreover, editorial theory has made important advances since the date of McKerrow's *Prolegomena*. Hence it would seem a necessity for an editor to formulate a fresh set of editorial principles both in respect to the treatment of the text and to the details of the apparatus.

It is not my purpose here to attempt this formulation or to survey the numerous minutiae of practical editorial problems on which McKerrow remained silent. For the first, I can say only that I believe the path lies through Greg's "Rationale of Copy-Text"; for the second, a growing experimentation has not yet produced a body of accepted doctrine. What I propose, instead, is to limit myself to one single topic—a selection from the things we need to know before we can produce the definitive edition of Shakespeare which we all desire. There are many ramifications which I must omit, and I shall be highly selective in illustration. Moreover, I propose to consider in any detail parts of only two specific problems: first, the importance of determining the nature of the manuscript behind any authoritative Shakespeare early printed text, in whole or in part; and, second, the closely allied subject of the bibliographical method which can be applied to assist in the solution of problems arising in the transmission of this copy from Shakespeare's autograph to print. The account will be one almost exclusively of difficulties, of information which we still need to secure and then to evaluate: the conclusion, that it will be a number of years before any editor can be prepared to publish a text which will have any pretensions towards definitiveness.

Time after time the problems in Shakespeare revert to the question, what was the nature of the copy behind the printed text and what has happened to that copy in the transmission to print. In present-day textual criticism this is the basic starting point for any enquiry, and many crucial considerations hinge on the double answer. Was the F1 *Hamlet* set from an independent manuscript, as Dover Wilson believes, [12] or from an annotated copy of Q2, 3, or 4, as Alice Walker has recently held?[13] Suppose we have a crux in the text in which F1 and Q2 agree. If the two texts were set from manuscripts which were truly different (and if Q2 came from Shakespeare's foul papers), the same reading found in two independently derived printed texts would serve powerfully to confirm it unless we were prepared to argue for an error in Shakespeare's autograph or for an identical misreading by F1 scribe and Q2 compositor, either of which is possible, of course. A typical case is the Q2-F1 concurrence in II.ii.181, "being a good kissing carrion," emended since the time of Warburton to "god

12 *The Manuscript of Shakespeare's* HAMLET *and the Problems of its Transmission* (Macmillan, 1934), I, 22 ff.
13 "The Textual Problem of *Hamlet*: A Reconsideration," *RES*, new ser., II (1951), 217-225.

kissing carrion," but of which Greg remarks, "[the emendation] is facile
and plausible, but I think unnecessary. Hamlet's fancies are not always as
nice as editors would have them."[14] Dr. Johnson thought "god kissing" to
be "a noble emendation, which almost sets the critic on a level with the
author"; and "god kissing" has persisted in Shakespeare's text to the present
day in the teeth of strong bibliographical evidence. There are many other
such possible 'improvements' in our traditional composite text of Shakespeare. Great as was Shakespeare's genius, once in a while a critic ought
to be able to surpass him in touching up an isolated image. Logically, if
one were to confine oneself only to the immediate case and its evidence,
there is every reason to suppose that "good kissing" was what Shakespeare
wrote and that it should appear in a bibliographical text in spite of the fact
that its subtlety is perhaps inferior to "god kissing." On the other hand,
there is almost certainly a connection here, which I think has not been
noticed before, with Q1 - Q2 concurrence in I.v.33, "That rootes it selfe
in ease on *Lethe* wharffe" where the Folio reads "rots." The case is very
complex, but I should say that if an editor reads "good" he must also read
"roots"; and if he emends to "god," he must correspondingly choose F
"rots."[15]

Yet if F1 were set from a quarto annotated by reference to some other
manuscript, as Alice Walker holds, concurrence of Q2 and F1 in the reading "good" would have much less validity, for the annotator could easily
have overlooked the variant (assuming that "god kissing" stood in the
manuscript being compared) and thus have failed to make the necessary
alteration in the quarto copy being marked for the F1 printer. If Dr.

---

14 *Principles of Emendation in Shakespeare* (reprinted from Proceedings of the British
Academy, vol. XIV. 1928), p. 68.

15 Proper discussion of these two cruces and the ramifications of the evidence concerning
them would go well beyond the confines of this paper, where my purpose is chiefly to
discuss principles and methods. The bibliographical implications of these two readings
are surveyed in my "A note on *Hamlet* I. v. 33 and II. ii. 181," forthcoming in the
Shakespeare Quarterly. Here I may say only this, that concurrence of Q2 and F1, though
strongly supporting any reading that makes tolerable sense, does not guarantee correct-
ness in all cases even though it places a considerable burden on an editor to demonstrate
the contrary, with especial reference to a credible reconstruction of how the double
error could have arisen. There are only two mechanical methods by which "good" can
be found by error in both Q2 and F1 (Q1 is here wanting) if the two texts were set
from different manuscripts, the Q2 copy being Shakespeare's foul papers. (1) A slip
of the pen by Shakespeare himself so that "good" actually stood in the autograph
although he had intended "god." To posit this mishap is second-guessing with a vengeance. In theory it could have happened, but no demonstration is possible, and the
pertinence of the *roots-rots* variant tells against it. (2) A seeming error in the manuscript was independently misread by Q2 compositor and prompt-copy scribe. I should
be inclined to argue for just such a case of double error in misreading handwriting in
the Q2-F1 concurrence in "bonds" at I. iii. 130 where I take it, with most editors, that
"bauds" (bawds) is the actual Shakespeare reading. But here the mistranscription of a
Secretary hand is much more readily explicable than the independent misreading of
single *o* as double *oo*. Again, the evidence of *roots-rots*, if pursued to its ultimate bibliographical conclusions, is against the hypothesis for double mistranscription of "god" as
"good." Where there are so many difficulties, we may well be left wondering whether
"good" and "roots" are not indeed what Shakespeare wrote.

Walker's hypothesis about the nature of the F1 copy could be demonstrated, an editor would be in considerable measure relieved from the logical restrictions which the first hypothesis imposes on his freedom to emend, and in such a case he might, perhaps, permit himself to be tempted by "god kissing carrion." This is only one of numerous examples where assumptions about the nature of the printer's copy have a most significant bearing on limiting or expanding the freedom permissible in the treatment of Shakespeare's text.

Let us assume with Dover Wilson, however, what seems more probable, that Q2 and F1 are independent. Which has the nearer transcriptional link with Shakespeare's autograph papers? If we can prove, as I am bound to say I think that Wilson has proved, at least in broad outline,[16] that Q2 was set directly from Shakespeare's foul papers, but that these foul papers had previously been transcribed by another hand to form the prompt copy, and this prompt copy in turn copied by still another scribe many years later to provide the printer with the manuscript for the Folio, then we have strong though far from perfect criteria for evaluating the variants between Q2 and F1. But there are further complications. It seems possible that some portion of the early scenes, and, doubtfully, the end, in Q2 was set either from an annotated copy of Q1, the bad quarto, or more likely, that some reference was made to Q1 even though the foul-papers manuscript was still the basic printer's copy. Here, when Q1 and Q2 agree but variance is found in F1, we are up against the problem whether the annotation of Q1 (if this was indeed the actual printer's copy) was complete and precise; and if not, whether the Folio preserves the genuine Shakespearian reading through failure of the scribe to alter the Q1 reading in the copy for Q2. On the other hand, if the printer consulted Q1 only on occasion for assistance in a doubtful reading, the authority of Q2 would be materially strengthened by this narrower limitation put on the possibility for contamination stemming from Q1. The general run of indifferent variants could be assigned with greater confidence to Folio sophistication, and the enquiry concentrated on the more unusual words which might have given trouble to the Q2 compositor.[17]

---

16 The statement is qualified because Wilson's failure to make a proper bibliographical analysis of his bibliographical evidence led him to offer unsubstantiated guesswork for ascertained fact. The weakness of his method is touched on below in connection with some remarks about compositorial study.

17 We must recognize, of course, that if the Q2 compositor consulted Q1 when he was in trouble over a word he could not conveniently guess at, the better reported lines of Q1 might give him the correct reading which he could confirm by re-examination of his manuscript. Nevertheless, we should be naive if we did not accept the probability that in cases where the Q1 reading could not possibly be fitted into the indecipherable letters of the manuscript, the Q2 compositor would not still adopt the different Q1 word in default of a better. At first sight, statistics suggest the possibility that we should give much more weight to the Folio variants in these early scenes than elsewhere when a manuscript can have been the only copy for Q2 or when consultation of the bad quarto

Variant readings for *Hamlet,* therefore, fall into six categories: (1) those in which Q1 and F1 agree against Q2; (2) those in which Q1 and Q2 agree against F1 in the lines where Q1 may have affected the Q2 copy; (3) those in which Q1 and Q2 agree against F1 when Q1 could no longer have influenced Q2; (4) those, if any, in which Q1 preserves a correct reading where both Q2 and F1 are corrupt; (5) errors common to Q2 and F1 where Q1 is absent; and (6) errors, if any, common to all three texts.[18]

In order to avoid unprincipled eclecticism an editor must group all variants into these six categories and then form a logically coherent theory to embrace any departures from the treatment which the evidence within and between these categories suggests. It is clear that Q1 agreeing, being absent, or independently varying, we are bound to accept any tolerable Q2 reading over a Folio variant (once Q1 ceases to influence Q2) unless we are prepared to demonstrate autograph error in the foul papers, compositorial error by the Q2 workman, or Shakespeare's authoritative revision in the prompt book at some point after transcription. Any one of these three factors could have entered for *Hamlet,* in theory,[19] and how to

_____

for doubtful readings seems to have been dropped. Greg (*Principles,* p. 60) lists 55 readings in which Q2 is joined by Q1 in disagreeing with F1. The figures, by acts, are 37, 6, 7, 1, and 4. Since the theory for the copy-influence of Q1 on Q2 for Act 1 had not been formulated when Greg wrote, he was able to remark only, "The fact that more than two thirds of the readings come from the first act must, I feel sure, have some important significance for the textual problem, but what this significance can be I am at present unable to imagine." The absence of the hypothesis for contamination, it should be pointed out, somewhat affects the validity of his subsequent analysis of these variants in the early scenes. If these statistics were to be taken literally, it would seem that in this part of the play about four of every five of the F1 variants are likely to be correct. Such an astonishing proportion might in fact obtain if annotated Q1 had been the printer's copy; but what evidence there is strongly suggests the contrary. Hence, if Q1 were used not for copy but only for consultation, we should expect the proportion of authoritative F1 variants to be considerably smaller. In such a case, the high percentage of variants concentrated in Act 1 could in part be accounted for by the fact that Q1 thereafter diverges more markedly from both Q2 and F1 so that the opportunities for its concurrence with Q2 against F1 are materially lessened and therefore the statistical proportion cannot be too narrowly applied. Nevertheless, we should not forget Greg's listing (p. 55) by acts of the variants in which Q1 and F1 agree against Q2, the figures being 20, 15, 14, 4, 4, the decline, as he suggests, "being naturally due to the greater divergence of Q1 towards the end of the play." If the figures here of 20, 15, 14 for the first three acts truly reflect the odds for concurrence, with especial relationship to the opportunities for Q1 to concur with either Q2 or F1, then the imbalance of 36, 6, and 7 for the agreement of Q1 and Q2 against F1 in these acts cannot be wholly explained away as due to the divergence of Q1 from both Q2 and F1 in the second and third acts as against the first act. Thus it would seem that the F1 variants in the first act must be given more weight than they merit later.

18 Slightly modified from Greg, *Principles,* p. 54. Greg also notices undoubtedly Shakespearian lines which appear in Q1 only, and also passages for which either Q2 or F1 is the sole authority.

19 Whether Shakespeare did or did not correct the prompt book following its transcription is a difficult though highly important enquiry for a textual critic. We may perhaps be suspicious of any hypothesis requiring two such stages of authorial correction, the second at a point some distance removed in time from the first. On the other hand, it may be critical rigidity to assume automatically that the players' parts were of necessity transcribed from the prompt book. Some interesting anomalies could be explained without requiring a second round of correction if we conjectured that the parts could have been transcribed from the foul papers for speed in getting the play into rehearsal before the prompt book itself was transcribed. From the Henslowe papers we know that this was occasionally done.

differentiate them is a serious problem if we are to avoid constructing a purely mechanical text for Shakespeare.

To steer a path through all the pitfalls of *Hamlet,* therefore, the anomalies within the six textual categories must be viewed in the light of fresh investigations of possible features in the handwriting of the first and second transcribers affecting readings in the Folio; the important question of scribal sophistication or of interference by the bookkeeper; the question of authoritative or unauthoritative intervention in prompt books to alter them in minor literary ways; the crucial determination of the exact relationship of Q1 to Q2; the question whether the players' parts were transcribed before or after the prompt book; and the minute analysis of the influence of the Q2 and F1 compositors on the transmission of the text. In some respects these are questions which involve a total study of all Shakespearian text, as well as that of other dramatists. No editor can tackle *Hamlet* until, in effect, he has edited all the other Shakespearian plays; and in all details he cannot edit the other plays until he has tackled *Hamlet.*

Various of these matters will no doubt always remain undemonstrable hypothesis although they are subjects for more rigorous study than has yet been given them, but the most fruitful positive results, perhaps, can accrue in an area not yet explored; that is, the technical study of the printing process for both Q2 and F1 to enable us to recover with a greater degree of certainty the manuscript reading, however genuine that may be in certain cases, behind the printed texts.

For all the detail of his monograph on the manuscript of *Hamlet,* this was a kind of evidence for which Dover Wilson substituted sheer guesswork instead of ascertained fact. A single illustration can be provided for each of the two texts. Wilson makes two assumptions about the compositor of Q2 which are very important for his theory: (1) only one compositor set the whole text; (2) this compositor was an untutored dolt who was setting difficult copy at a rate far beyond his normal speed. As proof for the first, that only one compositor set the text, he asserts that the imperfections are so uniformly distributed throughout that it is inconceivable they belong to two different workmen (I,98). This is not evidence or proof, for if the imperfections of the copy were responsible for the printed results there might well be a relatively even distribution of error. But convinced that the errors are compositorial, Wilson automatically accepts as authoritative various extra words supplied by the Folio, and then uses— with considerable circularity—the appearance of these words in the Folio as demonstration that they were missing in Q2. Even so shrewd a critic as Greg was misled in the early days by Wilson's argument into assigning a number of these readings as omissions in the quarto rather than as possible additions by the playhouse scribe.[20] One scientific way to determine the question would be to make a spelling test which would substitute fact for fantasy by actually determining whether one or more compositors were at work. This has not yet been done for Q2.

If the compositor of Q2 was the illiterate numbskull that Wilson makes him out to be, it is difficult to see how he was ever hired as a compositor. Wilson's confident statements that this compositor could memorize no more than one word at a time before turning to his cases is, of course, arrant nonsense and disproved by the very examples of anticipation which he provides. But it is of some importance to learn whether this compositor was in fact immoderately rushed in his typesetting, for such a theory has some bearing on the fidelity of his text. Wilson assumes that he was, on the evidence of his errors. But bibliographical evidence suggests the contrary. The details are too technical to offer here. Suffice it to say that certain assumptions can be made about the speed of presswork in relation to compositorial speed in early books on the evidence of the specific manner in which the type formes were imposed for the press, specifically on the evidence of the number of skeleton-formes constructed to hold the type-pages. I have made a preliminary analysis of these skeleton-formes in the Q2 *Hamlet* from the identification of the running-titles, and the results are very interesting. Sheets B, C, and D were imposed with a set of two skeletons for each sheet, this being a pattern customarily adopted when the compositor was comfortably ahead of the press. With sheet E two more skeletons were constructed, oddly enough, and thereafter the first set continues with sheets F and I while the new set imposes sheets G, H, K, and L. With sheets M, N, and O there is a curious mixture of the sets. This evidence suggests that composition speed was ahead of press speed, and there is even a question as to whether two presses were operating, in which case there must have been two compositors. Wilson's theory of the harried and driven workman does not appear to coincide with the picture given by bibliographical analysis of the physical facts of the printing. As a consequence, certain far-reaching conclusions he draws about the text may perhaps be wrong.

The case is no better for his consideration of the printing of the Folio text. In examining what he believes to be the remarkably higher percentage of error in the Folio *Hamlet* in comparison to *Antony and Cleopatra,* the purpose being to assign the error to the playhouse scribe and not to the Folio compositors, he writes, "So wide indeed is the disparity that, assuming as we legitimately may that the texts were set up by compositors who

---

20 *Principles*, p. 55.

were, if not the same workmen, workmen at least of similar efficiency, it can only be ascribed to a fundamental difference in the copies supplied them." And shortly, "In examining these items we must be careful to make generous allowance for the possibility of error on the part of the F1 compositors. Thus confusion of tense, person, number and mood in verbs, and confusion of number in nouns, are common types of compositors' misprint."

These are the words of a scholar who has not made the necessary bibliographical examination to determine his facts. We are aware from Dr. Willoughby's spelling tests (the theory for which was known some time before Wilson's monograph) that two compositors set the Folio *Hamlet* in rough alternation, and we know the precise columns of type set by these two workmen, A. and B. Further spelling tests establish that *Antony and Cleopatra* was set by only one compositor, the workman called B.[21] We have, then, some real basis for comparison in that these are two tragedies set from manuscript, one completely and one in part by the same workman. We can now approach the difference which I shall emphasize between the bibliographical approach to textual criticism which will be a desideratum in our ideal definitive text, and the essentially non-bibliographical approach adopted in this matter by Wilson.

In the first place, Wilson was content to write vague generalities about conventional compositorial errors, and since he had not envisaged the necessity to determine which compositor set *Antony and Cleopatra,* he was conveniently led to the unsubstantiated statement that both compositors of *Hamlet* and of *Antony* must have been equally expert.[22] The comparison is in fact worthless. Since Wilson did not make a spelling test for *Hamlet* he could not break down the incidence of error in the Folio text according to the lines set by A. and by B.; and hence he had no means of knowing whether A. was of equal competence or whether he was superior or even markedly inferior to B., and whether, let us say, a heavy proportion of error in the work of A. was not perhaps responsible for the over-all high percentage in *Hamlet.*[23] And since he did not trouble to ascertain

---

21 I. B. Cauthen, Jr., "Compositor Determination in the First Folio *King Lear," Studies in Bibliography,* V (1952).
22 By this reasoning we should arrive at the conclusion that the maligned compositor of Roberts' Q2 *Hamlet* must have been as expert as that one of Nicholas Okes' regular workmen who alone set Q1 of *King Lear,* since both were regular employees in a printing house; and that the even greater hash which Okes' workman made of *King Lear* was due to the more serious imperfections of his copy. This statement is very likely true but the reasoning is circular and the conclusion does not support Wilson's opinion of the Q2 *Hamlet* compositor and his ability.
23 Since this breakdown has not been made, pending conclusion of a study of compositor A. now in progress, my remarks here are only hypothetical to illustrate possibilities. But it is worth pointing out that two crucial assumptions made by Wilson are not based on bibliographical evidence. The unwarranted theory of constant compositorial error is used to argue for a higher incidence of error in *Hamlet.* Thus the ensuing inference that the error was chiefly scribal lacks positive demonstration that it was not composi-

that compositor B. set all of *Antony and Cleopatra,* he was not able to compare the assumed percentage of error for B. in *Hamlet* with B.'s assumed percentage in *Antony.*

This would have been at least an elementary investigation, but I should further point out that it would not satisfy strict bibliographical requirements, since in the absence of a control second text the basis for assuming error in *Antony and Cleopatra* is a literary and not a bibliographical one (how can we know errors are present which yet make sense?); and the basis for assuming error in F1 *Hamlet* is bibliographical only because of certain initial assumptions about the nature of the manuscript behind Q2. It is, therefore, hypothesis reared on hypothesis for *Hamlet,* and basically undemonstrated in *Antony.*

How would a bibliographer attack this problem? The method is relatively simple. One identifies the work of A. or of B. in those plays in which the Folio used a known printed quarto for copy with little or no editorial intervention. Since the printer's copy is known, one has an exact control for establishing the fact that variants in the Folio are compositorial. Classification of these variants will thereupon demonstrate not only the incidence of error in the work of A. and of B. but also the precise kinds of error in the departure from copy of which each was habitually guilty. This investigation has been made for compositor B. in connection with a study of the text of *King Lear.*[24] A corresponding study of compositor A. is now underway for application to the text of *Richard II.*[25] The correlation of these two investigations will provide us with a large body of exact information to apply to the Folio *Hamlet,* as well as to every Folio play. The Folio variants from Q2 can then be assessed, according as A. or B. set the F1 text, against a large body of precise information about the habitual characteristics of these two workmen as scientifically demonstrated in control plays. No editor of *Hamlet,* or of any Shakespeare play, has

---

torial. Various verbal anticipations in F1 *Hamlet* are put forward as further proof that the copy was scribal (specifically, an actor familiar with the play) on Wilson's bare statement that a compositor memorizes no more than four or five words at a time, and thus cannot anticipate words a line or two ahead. This is mere fantasy. In editing the plays of two such divergent playwrights as Dekker and Dryden I have found that one of the most common punctuational errors is the manifest transposition of pointing between two or even three lines, thus demonstrating that compositors, as one would normally expect, customarily carried several lines of verse in their heads while setting. Thus the major part of Wilson's examples of anticipation in support of his scribal theory is quite worthless as evidence.

24 I. B. Cauthen, Jr., unpublished University of Virginia dissertation now being prepared for dissemination in a series of articles.

25 R. E. Hasker, University of Virginia dissertation in progress. Before embarking on his research Mr. Hasker had to re-examine the question of the F copy of *Richard II.* His investigation has upset the theory held since the days of Pollard and has established that the copy was not Q5 but instead Q3 patched at the end by two leaves from Q5, doubtless another example of the theatrical use of a printed promptbook. See his "Copy for the First Folio *Richard II*," *Studies in Bibliography,* V (1952).

previously had this priceless information; but the new standard text will embody it of necessity.

While we are on the subject of the effects on the Folio text of the physical printing process and what we can learn from it to pierce the veil of print and bring us back to the relatively pure underlying manuscript, let me mention a further matter which is likely to delay for some years the completion of any definitive text until bibliographical facts are ascertained.

Until we know as a fact all the ascertainable details of the proof-reader's interference with the compositor's original typesetting in the Folio, no editor can dare to issue a Shakespeare text which relies in any way on Folio authority. No man's lifetime would be long enough to collate the preserved copies of the First Folio by hand in order to determine these variant readings. But Dr. Charlton Hinman has now perfected a most ingenious collating machine based on the principle of superimposition. It is to be hoped that within the next five years he will have collated his way through the seventy-nine Folger Shakespeare Library First Folios and that his results will later be made available for editorial purposes in an annotated new First Folio facsimile. Three actual First Folio proof sheets have turned up to give us some idea of the press-corrector's markings. Moreover, as a trial, Dr. Hinman has machine-collated all of the Folger Folios for *Othello*. From the evidence at hand it would seem that no very startling variants may be revealed to change our ideas of Shakespeare's text; but cumulatively, in small detail after small detail, the total result is sure to be significant.[26]

Two further plays may be mentioned which involve the twin problems of the precise determination of printer's copy and its transmission from Shakespeare's autograph, together with the effects of the printing process. In neither case is an editor as yet prepared to construct a text until these problems are solved. The plays are *Troilus and Cressida* and *Henry IV, Part 2*. I do not propose to attempt final answers for either, but merely to suggest the problems that must be worked out.

Troilus and Cressida was published in a quarto edition with a good text. The Folio version contains 33 full lines and a few part lines not found in Q, as well as a prologue. In addition, its text throughout exhibits further

---

26 Shakespeare editors have usually referred to only one copy of the First Folio for their text; moreover, the Lee facsimile has done heavy duty in this respect and only a few other prominent Folios have been utilized for textual purposes. Thus there has been very little opportunity to discover variants, and as it stands if an editor writes that the Folio reads thus and thus, all he can mean is that a particular copy has the reading. We cannot know what the Folio actually reads until we have complete information about all the variant states for each forme. This is the more important since press-corrected formes are likely to outnumber the uncorrected states by a heavy proportion; yet a bibliographical editor normally prefers the uncorrected state (misprints aside) as closer to the manuscript and free from the printing-house reader's sophistication.

signs of dependence upon some fresh authority, for by the latest count there are 507 substantive variants, or differences in wording, a number far too great to assign exclusively to compositorial change. For many years the argument has swung back and forth as to whether the Folio was typeset from an independent manuscript, or whether the printer's copy was the quarto itself, annotated by reference to a manuscript. Until this question was settled, no editor could have even the basis for constructing a text. Fortunately, Professor Williams has now demonstrated beyond the shadow of a doubt that the F1 copy was an annotated quarto.[27] However, this solution is only the first step towards editing, for there remains the further problem of determining the origin and authority of the Folio variants. Until that question is settled, an editor can have only his fallible literary taste to decide between the two forms of any variant reading. No principle of selection based on the external facts of the case is possible. Although some editors have felt the Folio to be generally superior, and others that the quarto was in general preferable, there is now some agreement that by and large the Folio readings are inferior.

This is an odd state of affairs and needs explanation, for it requires the Folio editors to have altered what seems to be a superior copy by the substitution of inferior readings. But it is not enough to trust to our literary taste in this matter. On the basis of both external and internal evidence we must conceive an acceptable hypothesis about this manuscript that was used to revise the quarto; and on the basis of this hypothesis then judge the Folio variants as a whole as well as in each particular. Did they come from a prompt copy, supposing one to have existed? In that case in some part they may represent scribal or theatrical alteration, and such readings would need to be distinguished and rejected. Did they come from Shakespeare's revised copy? If so, we must accept them, mechanical errors apart, regardless of our personal likes or dislikes. Did they come from an earlier manuscript of the play than that used as copy for the quarto? This is an interesting question which necessitates arriving at some acceptable hypothesis about the quarto manuscript, since the two problems will be related. Paradoxically, if the quarto could be demonstrated as printed from a superior and later-revised manuscript than that which produced the Folio variants, we might be justified in rejecting all F readings save those correcting manifest errors in Q.

No answer to these crucial questions has yet been fully worked out and published, but Dr. Williams has made interim reports before both the MLA and the Bibliographical Society of the University of Virginia in which he argued for the last hypothesis, that the Q manuscript was a

27 Philip Williams, "Shakespeare's *Troilus and Cressida*: the Relationship of Quarto and Folio," *Studies in Bibliography,* III (1950), 131-143.

revised autograph copy of the original foul papers from which the F variants were later drawn. Whatever the difficulties of explaining the precise circumstances by which this situation could have arisen, I have little doubt that he will be able to prove his case for the nature of the manuscripts.[28] So far so good. But the Shakespearian editor is not out of the woods yet. All cases of actual error in the quarto will not be manifest error. To believe that we can invariably detect a compositor's departure from copy because of memorial failure or orthographical misreading is to assume that he will set nonsense which can be identified. However, any student of texts knows that compositors have a fatal facility for making sense when they corrupt their copy, and that an editor's severest problem is to detect this plausible sense which is yet not the author's. Thus we cannot automatically assume that every word in the quarto is genuine Shakespeare, no matter what the copy, or that all the words are arranged in precisely the order in which Shakespeare wrote them in his manuscript. As a consequence, if we provisionally accept Dr. Williams' theory about the manuscripts, a Folio variant could conceivably come under any one of six different categories: (1) the variant in F may be an authentic Shakespearian reading, and that in Q may be an authentic Shakespearian reading, but the one may be early and the other a revision; (2) the F variant may be a scribal mistake or sophistication in annotation; (3) the F variant may be compositorial; (4) the F variant may be a genuine Shakespeare reading correcting a Q compositorial corruption; (5) there may be double error and the F and Q variants may each be wrong for various reasons; and (6) no variation may appear, but F may have failed to correct a Q corruption.

In each of these six cases the choice of reading is completely dependent upon the editor's ability to place the variant in the correct category; and until he has a method for assigning these variants by something other than guesswork, he cannot hope to achieve a scientific and definitive text. I do not anticipate that the bibliographical method will for each variant produce a definitive result. But I do suggest that a searching bibliographical enquiry —which has never previously been made for the *Troilus and Cressida* text—will provide a firmer foundation for decision than personal taste or any rigid theory giving absolute preference to one or other text.[29]

What I propose follows the lines of my suggestion to Dr. Cauthen for dealing with the *King Lear* problem, and his researches have shown that

---

28 Dr. Williams is proposing to publish his complete investigation in *Studies in Bibliography*, VI (1953).

29 In the case of divided authority between two texts but where one text could be shown to have been authoritatively revised, McKerrow (*Prolegomena*, p. 18) felt that an editor must accept *all* the variants in the revised edition save for those indubitably in error; but Greg (*RES*, XVII (1941), 140-141) has shown the fallacy of this view.

the method is practicable and valid. An editor will have gone a long way towards assessing the the textual variants if he can have some factual basis for isolating those readings in the Folio which were the compositor's from those which stood in the printer's copy. To do this a bibliographical editor would divide the *Troilus* Folio text between compositors A. and B. by the application of the spelling tests which have now been highly developed. He would then classify all variants between Q and F according to the known characteristics of whichever compositor set the F lines in question, these habitual departures from copy having been established by classification of the respective compositorial variants in plays where F was set from known printed copy which can act as a control. From this investigation it would be most surprising if some considerable proportion of the 500 odd Folio variants could not be isolated as compositorial. Ideally a similar compositor study would be made for the workman or men who set the quarto, to attempt to isolate those F variants which probably correct Q departures from copy. But even without this last step (more difficult to assess when there is no 'control') the problem would be greatly clarified. In *Troilus and Cressida*, fortunately, the problem is not nearly so difficult as in *Hamlet*, where the same method must be used, for the fact that we now know the Folio *Troilus* was set from the quarto itself causes a material simplification.

The other play is *Henry IV*, Part 2, and I shall be briefer since I am dealing only with a guess on which as yet I have done no investigation. Of all Shakespearian texts this, together with *Othello*, seems to present the most difficult problem about the nature of the printer's copy for the Folio, that crucial question which prevents any form of accurate editing until it is answered. In the New Variorum, Shaaber presents strong and very convincing arguments that F was set from an independent manuscript, almost certainly a scribal transcript of the prompt copy. In two recent articles Alice Walker summarizes and adds new arguments to the equally strong and convincing hypothesis that F was set from an annotated copy of Q.[30] Each side has striking evidence in its favor, but against each there is almost insurmountable evidence to show that it is wrong. Clearly something is amiss, for both hypotheses cannot simultaneously be right in any literal sense. It is evident, moreover, that we are faced with an extraordinary case, for in the past when proper methods have been applied there has been no difficulty in determining whether or not a Folio text derived from a manuscript or from an annotated quarto, as with *King Lear* and *Troilus and Cressida*, or *Hamlet* and *Othello*. Yet there is this trouble with

---

[30] "Quarto 'Copy' and the 1623 Folio: 2 *Henry IV*," *RES*, new ser., II (1951), 217 - 225. See also, "The Cancelled Lines in 2 *Henry IV*, IV. i. 93, 95," *The Library*, 5th ser., VI (1951), 115 - 116.

Henry IV, Part 2, and until we know the answer we cannot pretend to be able to edit it in any definitive and textually scientific manner.

I feel strongly that what is wrong with this play cannot be explained by either of the two conventional hypotheses. Both present such indubitable evidence in their favor that both must be right only in part, and some fresh hypothesis must be advanced which will reconcile the completely opposed sets of evidence. I suggest tentatively, subject to an investigation I plan for the near future, that both Shaaber and Walker are right and that both are wrong. Both a new manuscript and the quarto were in fact used for copy. The answer must logically be that for some reason an annotated quarto was transcribed to form a manuscript which was used as printer's copy for the Folio. This could have happened if at some time antecedent to the printing of the Folio the manuscript prompt copy wore out and was replaced as prompt book by a copy of the quarto, annotated by comparison with the old manuscript before it was discarded. The company would not wish to relinquish this sole remaining copy to the Folio printer if the play were still in repertory; but the foul papers were not available to serve as a substitute, for they had been used up in printing the quarto, as Shaaber has demonstrated. Hence the only way of providing copy for Jaggard was to transcribe the prompt book, as was done for *Hamlet.* In this case, however, the prompt book was the quarto, and thus we have the anomaly of *2 Henry IV.* This is what logic seems to dictate. The problem will be to find the evidence.

It is time to add up the balance sheet and to indicate the editorial problem for Shakespeare as a whole. We have seventeen plays (eighteen, if we deny the Shakespearian origin of *A Shrew*) which appeared in the Folio for the first time and for which, therefore, we possess only one authoritative text. These are 1 *Henry VI, The Comedy of Errors, Two Gentlemen of Verona, King John, Julius Caesar, As You Like It, Twelfth Night, All's Well that Ends Well, Measure for Measure, Macbeth, Antony and Cleopatra, Coriolanus, Timon of Athens, Cymbeline, The Winter's Tale, The Tempest,* and *Henry VIII.* For each of these, as for all plays later to be considered where F has any independent authority, the press-variants made during the course of printing F must be ascertained, the compositors identified, and the text scrupulously examined in the light of these known compositors' characteristics.[31] Furthermore, current hypotheses about the nature of the copy underlying each text must be re-examined, and confirmed or revised, this also holding true for all remaining plays. It makes a great deal of difference to an editor faced with a textual

---

31 The anomalous sections of the Folio which have not as yet been associated either with A. or B. will need working out to determine whether a third workman or pair of compositors had a hand in the typesetting.

crux whether he knows that the printer's copy was Shakespeare's own papers or else a Ralph Crane transcript of a theatrical prompt book, itself in all probability a transcript of Shakespeare's foul papers. We need to know much more about the mechanical reasons for such irregular verse lining as we find in *Coriolanus* and whether Professor G. B. Harrison is right that this reflects Shakespeare's own late practise. Regrettably, we must lay various ghosts which Dr. Flatter has raised, in my opinion fallaciously, about the significance of the versification and punctuation of Shakespeare text as a direction to the actors.[32]

We have five plays (perhaps only four, dependent upon our view of *A Shrew*) which exist in bad quartos but for which the F printer's copy was a good manuscript with no transcriptional link whatsoever to the manuscript behind the quartos. These are 2 & 3 *Henry VI, The Taming of the Shrew* (if we accept this as having a bad quarto), *Henry V*, and *The Merry Wives of Windsor*.[33] The problem is essentially the same as for the first group, except that the bad quarto is very occasionally of some assistance as a control.

Two plays exist in which the Folio printer's copy was a bad quarto revised and annotated by comparison with a manuscript in the possession of the theatrical company. These are *Richard III* and *King Lear*. The prime problem is to attempt to separate the scribal annotations from the compositorial variants by means of a compositor analysis, and thus to arrive as close as possible to a reconstruction of the annotated printer's copy itself. Thereafter, since we may suppose the scribe did not invariably correct all bad quarto errors and, in addition, doubtless made some annotations in a form different from that in the manuscript, the text must be attacked from the point of view of pure textual criticism. This criticism, having the advantage of a recovery of the lost printer's copy, can then proceed to disentangle the scribal lapses both of omission and of commission.[34] For these two plays the Folio will serve as the copy-text for the accidentals and will have major substantive authority.

We have eight plays in which the Folio printer's copy was an unrevised reprint of a good quarto text. These are *Titus Andronicus, Love's Labours*

---

[32] See my review of *Shakespeare's Producing Hand* in *MP*, XLVIII (1950), 64 - 68. The new Arden *Macbeth*, unfortunately, has been influenced by these theories, which are bibliographically unacceptable and are not supported by true and complete evidence.

[33] The bad-quarto theory for Q1 of *The Merry Wives* (and, if I understand him correctly, for all Shakespearian bad quartos at least as concerns their derivation from memorial reconstruction) has recently been challenged by Dr. Bracy in a monograph on *The Merry Wives* text for the University of Missouri Studies. But in my opinion his arguments are more pejorative than convincing, and he seems to exhibit little idea of what constitutes scholarly evidence.

[34] One of the few criticisms it is possible to make of G. I. Duthie's recent critical edition, of *King Lear* (Blackwell, 1949) is that he had no bibliographical method for determining compositorial departure from copy in the F1 text. This has now been supplied by I. B. Cauthen's researches. Mr. Duthie, also, was unaware of the press-variants in the F text.

Lost, Romeo and Juliet, Richard II, A Midsummer-Night's Dream, The Merchant of Venice, I *Henry IV,* and *Much Ado About Nothing.* Of these *Titus Andronicus* contains a new scene first present in the Folio, and *Richard II* a scene for which the Folio offers the only authoritative text. *Romeo and Juliet* presents a special problem in view of the fact that there is something peculiar in connection with the transcription of the manuscript which served as printer's copy for the good quarto, Q2; and the Q2 text has some relation to the Q1 bad quarto.[35] With all these plays the earliest good quarto must be the copy-text and major authority for the substantives. However, an editor must attempt to determine by a compositor analysis of the Folio text which of the Folio variants have authority, if any, and which are compositorial.

Hamlet and *Othello* constitute the only two plays in which both F and Q were, according to the traditional view, set up from different good manuscripts. In considering *Hamlet* I have already touched upon the serious editorial problem which results from this situation, although the conditions are such that in theory, at any rate, an editor should be able to recover the maximum genuine text of Shakespeare. According to the commonly accepted theory of the history of the manuscripts underlying each text, in both cases the quarto would serve as copy-text but readings from the Folio, once these have been distinguished from the Folio compositors' lapses, need to be seriously considered on their merits, variant by variant, in the light of the manuscript theory.

Pericles presents a hopeless problem with only a bad-quarto text available in the original edition and its reprints.

Finally, if I am even approximately right in my speculations about 2 *Henry IV,* we have one play in which a good quarto exists and the Folio printer's copy was a scribal transcript of an annotated printed copy used as a prompt book. In this case Q1 should be the copy-text and the general authority for the substantives. In the Folio text compositorial and scribal variants need to be sifted in an attempt to recover any readings, variant from the quarto, which came directly from the discarded playhouse manuscript. These then need examination, variant by variant, to determine whether they represent more authoritative readings than those in the quarto.

Few if any of the editorial decisions I have sketched can be made in connection with any isolated single play: all plays contain certain basically similar problems which have a bearing on solutions applied to any indi-

---

35 The most complete survey of the problems of the Q2 text is found in an interim report by G. I. Duthie, "The Text of Shakespeare's *Romeo and Juliet," Studies in Bibliography,* IV (1951), 3 - 29. His forthcoming edition of the play in the New Cambridge series will offer his final conclusions.

vidual text. Clearly, we cannot expect our definitive text to be the result of editorial collaboration. Only one man can be responsible, since only one man can have the necessary close experience with any play simultaneously to apply his results to another. And only one man in such delicate matters can even attempt the consistency of approach and level standards which are a prime necessity. Moreover, this editor, though requiring some mechanical assistance, will need to be in the thick of the doings. No mere director, or general editor, acting only in a supervisory capacity can expect to gain the intimate knowledge, much less the invaluable feel for his material which seems intuitive but is in truth semi-conscious accumulated experience.

When this huge task is accomplished, what shall we have? No one should expect a miracle. The famous textual cruces have been battered about for so long that if the genuine reading is recoverable short of calling Shakespeare up from the dead, it has already been found out—if only we could be sure which one of the various alternatives it is. In some few of these cases the accumulated bibliographical information which has been denied every other editor may help materially towards a correct choice from among the possibilities. But certain cruces are not susceptible to scientific bibliographical solution and must always rest on inspired and sympathetic imagination, undemonstrable but seemingly inevitable.[36] Literary criticism is not excess baggage in a bibliographical editor, nor is a linguistic knowledge, which is perhaps the greatest weakness in editors of Elizabethan texts, who are usually helpless when the *NED* is silent.

We cannot, therefore, expect this new standard text to be consistently different in any sensational manner from what we have been accustomed to reading. But I am sure there can be no question that small point after small point, which in some plays will rise to a cumulatively powerful total, the text will present a truer picture of what superior method and experience can confirm and recover of Shakespeare's actual words in their correct order and context than anything we have available now or can anticipate in the near future. It is unlikely that any major literary theories will be overturned by a new text. But we shall at least have the satisfaction of knowing that subsequent criticism,[37] to say nothing of our own reading pleasure and understanding of Shakespeare, will be based—no matter how minute the point—on a text that is as much a certainty as the accumulated experience of at least two generations of a new textual tradition is capable of constructing.

UNIVERSITY OF VIRGINIA.

---

36 Always provided these inspired reconstructions, like Theobald's "babbled of green fields," are check-reined by the bibliographical history of the texts. See the comments on "god kissing" above.
37 And, hopefully, a new concordance and grammar.

Simms's Edition of the Shakespeare Apocrypha

by EDD WINFIELD PARKS

I N 1848 WILLIAM GILMORE SIMMS, according to his biographer, "finally succeeded in having published" a book which today has at least *curiosa* interest: *A Supplement to the Plays of William Shakespeare*.[1] Although Simms's *Supplement* was the first edition of the Shakespearian Apocrypha prepared by an American, W. P. Trent devotes only a scant half-paragraph to the book, calling the editor's work "slight both in quantity and in quality," but adding that the work was undertaken "as a labor of love" and was another manifestation of Simms's steady and enthusiastic reading of Elizabethan dramas.[2]

The most recent editor of the apocryphal plays, C. F. Tucker Brooke, lists all of Simms's textual conjectures in his footnotes, and discusses some of the more and some of the least plausible ones in the section of notes after the plays.[3] Brooke dismisses most of these rather cavalierly and with some justice, for Simms lacked the scholarship and the books to handle textual problems adequately. He does not describe Simms's method, but it is easily discernible: he selected as his basic text the work of Charles Knight for *The Two Noble Kinsmen* and *A Yorkshire Tragedy,* and the edition of Malone for the five other plays. But he was no slavish follower. He levied upon Theobald, Seward, Mason, and Weber for emendations and for variant readings which he gave in footnotes; and he did not hesitate

---

1 *A Supplement to the Plays of William Shakespeare: comprising the seven dramas, which have been ascribed to his pen, but which are not included with his writings in modern editions, namely*: THE TWO NOBLE KINSMEN; THE LONDON PRODIGAL; THOMAS, LORD CROMWELL; SIR JOHN OLDCASTLE; THE PURITAN, OR THE WIDOW OF WATLING STREET; THE [*sic*] YORKSHIRE TRAGEDY; THE TRAGEDY OF LOCRINE. Edited, with Notes, and an Introduction to each Play, by William Gilmore Simms. New York, 1848. A second edition was published in 1855. Both editions were copyrighted by George F. Cooledge and Brother. The 1848 title-page lists the book as "Published by George F. Cooledge and Brother, Booksellers and Publishers, 323 Pearl Street, 1848." The 1855 edition has two title-pages, although otherwise it was printed from the plates of the first edition. It was brought out, presumably simultaneously, with one title page reading: "Philadelphia: Published by Jas. B. Smith & Co., No. 146 Chestnut Street, 1855." The other title page indicates a cooperative publishing venture: "Auburn and Rochester: Alden and Beardsley. New York: J. C. Derby, 119 Nassau Street. 1855." The bindings are different, and the New York edition was printed on much heavier and more expensive paper, with a frontispiece portrait of Shakespeare.

2 William P. Trent, *William Gilmore Simms* (Boston, 1892), 310. Trent does not explain why Simms had difficulties in getting the book published.

3 *The Shakespeare Apocrypha*, edited by C. F. Tucker Brooke (Oxford, 1908), 425, 426 (where he calls Simms a "blind follower" of Malone), 433-35. In his edition of fourteen plays Brooke includes the seven selected by Simms.

to make changes of his own, although he was scrupulous about noting all of these changes.

He notes explicitly one change in *The Two Noble Kinsmen* about which he had consulted Knight: in II, 3, he makes Arcite's speech read

and run, —

> Swifter the wind upon a field of corn
> (Curling the wealthy ears) ne'er flew.

Simms wrote of this: "with Mr. Knight's permission, I have ventured to restore the reading of *the* for *than,* with a new punctuation, preferring, though with great deference, the present construction to his own."[4] He was a modest editor, and as far as conjectures and variants go, a reliable one.

Unfortunately he accepted Knight's expurgations, and bowdlerized on his own hook, with the excuse that

> Our edition is for general readers, as well as for critical students. The essential difference between Shakespeare and Fletcher makes it necessary to adopt a different course with reference to the two writers. It is not a false reverence for Shakespeare that calls upon an editor to leave his text unchanged; but a just discrimination between the quality of what is offensive in him and in other writers of his age . . . I see no reason to disturb the opinions or depart from the rule that Mr. Knight has prescribed for himself, in the exclusion of offensive passages.[5]

Although he believed *Locrine* to be by Shakespeare, he does not hesitate to omit "simple" or "offensive" grossness. In III, 4, he stops William's speech

> Marry, Sir, what reason had you when my
> sister was in the barn to —

omitting the words

> tumble her upon the haie, and to fish her belly.[6]

The expurgations are carefully noted in all the plays, but they make the texts worthless for the critical student or the general reader. In accepting the custom of his own day the editor limited this part of his work to that day, for he did not give us complete texts.

His critical introductions should not be dismissed so lightly. They have continuing interest, and some value, for they present an examination of the plays from the point of view of an experienced creative writer.

Simms's exclusions are severe. He accepted for his book only the seven plays "which have (wholly or in part) been ascribed to his pen, and

---

4 Simms, *A Supplement,* 25. He followed the same policy with Malone's texts.
5 Simms, 37.
6 Simms, 169. Other typical deletions appear on 165 and 173.

included, at an early period, among his works."[7] But he was not unmindful of the claims advanced in later times "by ingenious criticism" for the inclusion of other plays, and he half-promises that a group of these, "the ascription of which to William Shakespeare rests chiefly upon opinion," might be the matter for an additional volume. It was never published, and presumably never edited. But Simms's brief judgments upon these plays are worth quoting, as much for what he voluntarily reveals of his own ignorance as of his critical opinion. This group of excluded plays

> comprises "Arden of Feversham"—a piece of considerable merit; "the reign of King Edward III."—a work so like Shakespeare's, in the respects of versification and manner, that it is difficult to hit upon any writer who could so happily have imitated him; "George a-Greene, the Pinner of Wakefield"—which is now supposed to have been written by Robert Greene, but upon the most slender of all sorts of evidence; "Fair Emma" [sic]—which Mr. Knight assigns to a period subsequent to the death of Shakespeare; "Mucedorus," of which we know nothing, and can express no opinion,—Tieck and Horn, the German critics, pronounce it a youthful production of Shakespeare; Mr. Knight gives us a brief analysis of the story, describes it as a lively play, with some few passages of merit, but, otherwise, speaks of it slightingly;—"The Birth of Merlin"—which in its first known edition, that of 1662, was announced as the joint production of Shakespeare and Rowley; and "The Merry Devil of Edmonton"—a performance which, as Mr. Knight justly remarks, is that of a true poet, whoever he may be."[8]

If Simms knew or had seen Alexander Dyce's edition of *Sir Thomas More* (1844) he does not mention it, although he dedicated his collection to Dyce; by the standards expressed above, Simms would have excluded it from his own work. Except for *Sir Thomas More,* he was at least cognizant of the claims for all the plays included by Tucker Brooke, and the only one that he added to Brooke's list was *George a-Greene.* Simms may have leaned heavily on the critical opinions of other men, but his list was conservative and sensible.

II

His approach to the authenticity of individual plays was also conservative, but his approach to the general problem was bold and original. He had received little formal education, and no training in scholarship. But he had read widely and studiously, especially in the field of the Shakespearian drama, and he had made for himself a reputation as a distinguished novelist, a capable poet, and a vigorous critic. Aware of his own short-

---

[7] Simms, 12.
[8] Simms, 12.

comings, he was also aware of his achievements. His approach, then, was that of the creative writer, not that of the scholar; although he recognized the immense superiority of Shakespeare, he felt that the greater author had in his time surmounted many of the problems that he himself had once faced and only partially solved.

From that point of view, and with a backward glance at his own experience, Simms is willing to admit that a youthful genius may turn out much bad work:

> We have said that the deficiency of these works . . . is by no means to be admitted as an argument against their legitimacy. The opinion is not entertained without serious deliberation. The truth is, that a young author seldom writes from himself at first. He is more apt to write like anybody but himself. He subdues and suppresses himself. He does not feel himself. He is compelled to look out of himself for models and authorities, before he can properly unfold himself . . . This very unfolding of self is the great business of life—never wholly effected, even with the utmost diligence, until the author has reached the mellow period of middle life, and seldom even then.[9]

Out of his own experience Simms was convinced that even the youthful Shakespeare was both imitative and derivative. He thought it a sufficient test of worth if he could find in a play by a very young man "an occasional germ which betrays freshness." But Simms's idea of just how young the author of some pieces may have been is a bit breath-taking. He is convinced that Shakespeare may have started writing by the time he was fifteen or sixteen, and that he had completed *Locrine* and *Titus Andronicus* by the time he went to London, "in his twenty-third year."

Simms's reasoning is at least plausible. The poetic germ, he notes, usually takes virulent hold upon a potential writer in his fifteenth year; although we do not know that Shakespeare started that early, it would be "a strangely unreasonable supposition" to believe that a man so prolific in his later career led "a vegetable life in Stratford." Here he drew upon his own experience. At the age of eight he was celebrating in verse the American victories over the British in the War of 1812, and according to his biographer "his pen was rarely idle, and his brain never" in the years that followed. His first book was published when he was nineteen; Trent suspects that many other youthful effusions found a place in later volumes, and a play was about this time accepted, rehearsed, and announced, although never produced. But Simms knew that his own early work was derivative: he was echoing the thoughts of others instead of speaking his own mind.[10] Simms may well have thought he was being very conservative when he suggested fifteen or

---

9 Simms, 7.
10 Trent, *Simms,* 7, 45-47.

sixteen as a likely age for the composition of *Locrine* or other apocryphal plays.

Simms draws a clear line between the plays that the boy Shakespeare might have written, and those which are the work of a mature person. The tests to be applied are entirely different. *A London Prodigal* is crude "as a work of thought and as a work of art." It is the work of an apprentice hand, and for that reason the usual tests are unreliable. Simms does not commit himself, but in spite of the authority of Malone and Knight he does not reject Shakespeare's authorship, but mildly favors it: The play

> exhibits a very immature condition of mind on the part of the writer. The invention, the verse, and the philosophy, are equally humble. It was probably the work of a youth—perhaps a boy—and that boy might have been Shakespeare. We know nothing more utterly absurd than this habit of testing the authorship of a work by its intrinsic merits; applying the standards formed in the maturer exhibitions of a great genius, to the crude and feeble performances of his beginning.[11]

He applies the same reasoning to *Locrine*. In his customary fashion, he quotes or summarizes the opinions of other scholars, and laments that he does not have available any of the works of Wentworth Smith, so that he could determine for himself whether or not Smith wrote *Locrine* and *Titus Andronicus*. Simms is certain that one man wrote both plays; he dissents sharply from Knight when the English critic concludes that the characteristics of *Locrine* are the reverse of Shakespeare because, as Simms summarizes, the characters "speak rather out of books, than because of their passions; because of the large amount of classical and mythological imagery which Locrine employs; the pedantry of the author; his frequent repetition of phrases, in order to be rhetorical and forcible; and other like platitudes, which need no more particular designation."[12] The faults which led Knight to deny Shakespeare's authorship are to Simms telling points in favor of that authorship. He holds each item to be characteristic of a youthful author, and he is convinced that *Locrine* is the work of a beginner, who still sets an exorbitant value on his school classics and is more interested in utterance than in character.

Once again Simms was writing out of his own experience. The chief employment of the young poet was mastering the arts of utterance, "an

---

11 Simms, 45-46.

12 Simms, 153. The next quotation is on the same page, and the long one from pp. 153-54. Although the question of the authorship of *Titus Andronicus* does not fall within the scope of this paper, it is pertinent to note that Simms's general remarks (not of course his quotations) are just as pertinent to *Titus* as to *Locrine*, and in fact answer beforehand many of the objections to including that play in the Shakespeare canon. G. L. Kittredge, *The Complete Works of Shakespeare*, 971-72, although preferring a later date than Simms gave ("1592 or 1593, with preference for 1592") accepted the authorship without any quibbling: "Shakespeare must have the credit as well as the discredit of its authorship."

acquisition which must inevitably precede the knowledge of character, and the philosophy which discriminates it happily." The faults of *Locrine* and of *Titus Andronicus* are the same, and they are faults typical of youth: an excess of bloody and brutal moods; an untamed and unmeasured ferocity; a tedious sameness of tone, unsparing resentments, and horrible purposes, which are left totally unrelieved by the redeeming interposition of softer fancies—of pity, or hope, or even love. In point of style and expression, the resemblance of faults between the two is even more decided . . . . we have the same frequent repetition of phrases, either to intensify the sound by reiteration, or to patch out an imperfect line—the same free use of heathen mythology—and the same frequent employment of fragmentary lines of Latin, either incorporated with, or closing the paragraph. The structure of the verse of "Titus Andronicus" is singularly like that of "Locrine." They are both full and sounding, and ample always to overflow in the rhythm. The sense is usually clear and transparent, and the energy of the lines is quite remarkable, showing a strength and resource in the author, in one of the first essentials of his art, infinitely in advance of those acquisitions of knowledge and thought which can only result from constant attrition and frequent experience with the world of man. This goes to prove the immature years of the author. The inequalities which he exhibits are precisely such as mark the productions of all youthful poets of genius, showing a more perfect mastery over versification than thought—showing the utterance more malleable than the idea.[12]

As Simms noted frankly, he concurred with the German critics, especially Tieck and Schlegel, and disagreed with most of the English. He made no attempt to compare *Locrine* with *Selimus,* and disregards the possibility that the play may have been written by Peele or Greene.[13] He believed the play to be written by Shakespeare, and that the phrase on the title page, "Newly set foorth, overseene and corrected by W. S.", meant simply that Shakespeare had slightly re-touched a play which he had written in Stratford. It is the only play that he positively attributes to Shakespeare, among the seven; he quotes at length to show that many verses have the authentic ring of the Master. The characteristics of Shakespearian verse, he decided, were manifest in

the usually abrupt manner in which the persons of the drama enter upon the business of the scene: in the noble comparisons and figures which suggest themselves, as if without effort or premeditation, to the speaker; in the presence of an overflowing and exuberant imagination; in the occasional reflection which the contemplative mood acknow-

---

13 On this point, see Tucker Brooke, XV-XX. Brooke does not mention Simms's contentions.

ledges, even in the moment of action and performance; and in that genius which frequently snatches its grace beyond the reach of art, in the felicitious expression, the happy phrase, the bold figure, the delicate and unique fancy.[14]

These are loose criteria, leaving Simms dependent on his mind and ear, and on his own training as a poet. The quotations are excellently selected to buttress the generalized characteristics that Simms has picked out as typical of Shakespeare. He makes his points clearly and well, but he is a judge who has already decided upon the verdict, and concentrates mainly on the evidence which confirms his view.

He was willing to accept as Shakespeare's any of the plays that seemed the work of an apprentice. He was not willing to accept work which "shows the familiarity of a master with his tools". *The Two Noble Kinsmen* he recognized as a mature work, by one or more able craftsmen; he is willing enough to assign it to Fletcher, and to admit that the opening scene is worthy of Shakespeare. But he disagrees with Pope, Coleridge, Lamb, and the German critics and denies that Shakespeare could have had any part in it because the

versification is not his. In spite of what Mr. Lamb has said on this subject, it lacks his flow and vivacity. The great marks of Shakespeare are his equal profundity and lucidity. He rises always with a wing from his subject, however low that may be, as we see birds skim along the surface of the ground, just above and without touching it. His most difficult thoughts, ordinarily, are those which flow musically; and the more comprehensive the range of his passions and ideas, they seem to choose for themselves an utterance of special clearness in due degree with the natural obstacles of the conception. Now, let the reader examine the metaphysical verse of the Two Noble Kinsmen, and he will see what embarrassments occur to the utterance of the writer in proportion to the subtlety of the sentiment.[15]

Simms had no knowledge of metrical tests or word analyses; he does not discuss such stylistic features as the typically Shakespearian coined words, archaistic words, unliterary words in Act I, Scenes 1-3, or in III, 1, or in V, 1, 3, 4. Possibly he would have thought these tests (which have seemed convincing to E. K. Chambers, G. L. Kittredge and, among others, the present writer[15]) too mechanical to be of much value. As in judging *Locrine,* he depended on a professionally trained mind and ear. It is inter-

---

[14] Simms, 154. His supporting quotations follow, 154-58.

[15] Simms, 13-14. A good summary is given by E. K. Chambers, *William Shakespeare,* I, 531-32. Kittredge, in *The Complete Works of Shakespeare,* 1409. says flatly: "The ascription to Fletcher and Shakespeare in the title page is undoubtedly correct." Although it is of no importance, R. C. Beatty and I included the play as representative of Shakespeare as a collaborator in *The English Drama 900-1642* (New York, 1935), because we believed Shakespeare's part in the play to be definitely established.

esting to note that Tucker Brooke, after summarizing Littledale's metrical tests and after calling the roll of critics who have advocated or denied Shakespeare's collaboration, falls back upon an equally subjective judgment:

> It is highly improbable that any critical reader of this play has met with a single scene which, after judging it on its own merits, he has been able to pronounce candidly and with absolute confidence to be the work of Shakespeare . . . . when we consider individually the parts of *The Two Noble Kinsmen* which have been ascribed to Shakespeare, we find invariably that each act, scene or verse falls just short of what it should be. Always there is the strong Shakespearian reminiscence, but nowhere quite the full and perfect reality that we could swear to.[16]

In spite of some weasel words, this is a strong statement. But it really only rephrases the arguments of Simms, with less convincing wording—and yet Simms is not listed in the roll-call of twenty-three scholars. The omission seems a bit ungracious, for Brooke is at least as close to Simms in point of view as to any other critic.

Simms felt secure in his own judgment of the play. He freely recognized its worth, but he recognized also the maturity of its authors, and he would not admit that the mature Shakespeare could have had a hand in it. He was willing to accept weak and even fumbling work from the apprentice, but not gorgeously uneven work from the master. He did not demand that all of Shakespeare's plays be of uniform excellence, based on standards determined by his finest work, but did demand a promise and a spark, and indications of youthfulness.

Since he could find none of these in *Thomas Lord Cromwell*, he dismissed it quickly as "a very feeble effort, almost totally deficient in poetry, and lamentably wanting as a work of art."[17] *Sir John Oldcastle* presented a more serious problem, for the play had considerable merit:

> The poetry is sometimes forcible and fine, if not rich and generous. It lacks the glow, the fire, the invention of Shakespeare, when on the wing, but possesses his frankness, impulse, and transparency. When Ulrici speaks of the unknown author of this play as imitating Shakespeare, or modelling himself upon him, he probably confounds two things, in their nature very different. It appears to me that, while the author of Sir John Oldcastle has appropriated certain of Shakespeare's materials, some two or more of his characters, and some of his incidents he has, neither in the plan of his story, nor in the structure of his verse, imitated any writer. His style of expression seems to be that of a practised writer, confident of his own mode of utterance . . . .[18]

---

16 Brooke, XLII-XLIII.
17 Simms, 67-68.
18 Simms, 88-89.

A bit reluctantly, since he admired the play, Simms ruled it out. He was not too much troubled by the entry in Henslowe's Diary "to pay Mr. Monday, Mr. Drayton, Mr. Wilson, and Mr. Hathaway" for the first part, and as earnest for the second part. Simms quotes the passage, but he feels that the "very employment of no less than four hands, in the preparation of this play, would seem to declare some present emergency."[19] If four hands were required, he would be willing to concede an unlisted fifth— but he did not believe that additional collaborator, if he existed, to be Shakespeare.

The Puritan belonged to an intermediate stage, and did not interest him. He was willing to follow Malone in consigning it to William Smith, or to admit it to the canon of Ben Jonson's inferior works; he mentions Dyce's identification of George Pyeboard with George Peele, purely for the reader's information; but though he noted again that maturity and strength in Shakespeare's unquestioned works were among the strongest arguments for believing in the existence of unacknowledged works, *The Puritan* was not among them.[20]

III

Simms did not pretend to himself or to his readers that he had solved any problems. His purpose in editing the works was primarily to persuade readers to share his own enthusiasm for the Elizabethan and Jacobean drama; although not averse to receiving credit for his knowledge or labor, he was at all times generously willing to lend his own prestige and popularity to the task of popularizing good but neglected work. His function as editor was first of all to make these plays accessible to readers. At the beginning of his General Introduction he stated explicitly that neither he nor the publishers proposed to decide upon the authenticity of the plays; this ticklish question would be left to "future criticism and the sagacity of the reader." He was more concerned that readers should become familiar with the merits of the plays than bogged down with problems of authorship.

In spite of this attitude, Simms perhaps inevitably devotes much of his own writing to the problem of authorship. His convictions on the subject were definite, and definitely stated. Even the greatest genius must go through a period of apprenticeship. His early works might be changelings or sons of premature birth, brought into the world before their time; they were not subject to the same tests as the "true heir" of the mature writer's labor. Yet their imperfections did not mean that they necessarily were outside the family, or that they should be consigned to oblivion. The genuine student or the youthful writer might even learn more of the pro-

---

19 Simms, 87-88.
20 Simms, 117-18.

cesses of dramatic construction from these imperfect and sometimes obvious efforts than he could from something approaching perfection.

Simms objected to the criticism, best exemplified in the work of Coleridge, that could admit no weaknesses or human flaws in Shakespeare. He was quite willing to admit that in the mature work Shakespeare's artistry was equal to his genius, but not to admit that either the artistry or the genius had burst forth in full flower. His own common sense, his own experience of writers and writing made him flatly certain that this was impossible. He realized that early work may have been lost or destroyed, but it once existed. That is the basis of his argument.

It is a liberal but tenable position. Simms assuredly does not convince us that any single play should be added to the Shakespeare canon, but he does tellingly present an argument that may too much have been neglected, in our concern with scholarly methods of testing for authorship. The writer must learn his trade, whether he be a genius or a hack, and the work of the learner is only the foundation on which the man builds; it may have few characteristics of the building. But it must exist. Simms had learned this from years of personal effort, and for that reason he believed that even Shakespeare must have learned it also. Plays that betrayed the marks of the beginner might or might not be by Shakespeare, but the novelist and poet felt that we ruled them out wrongly by comparing them with the great plays. It is quite possible that he is right, although not in individual instances as much as in his general thesis.

UNIVERSITY OF GEORGIA

Patriotism and Satire in Henry V

by ALLAN GILBERT

TO MAKE *HENRY V* a patriotic play is not an invention by Moviedom.

Before the Boer War, one editor wrote:

If we now compare Henry's antagonists [the French nobles] with himself, we shall see a dramatic contrast of the most striking kind, the contrast between pretence and reality—boasting and modesty— trust in numbers and trust in God. This contrast is most marked in the person of the Dauphin, but it holds also with the French in general . . . Aristocratic insolence, idle chatter, vaunting of numbers and armor and horses, this on the one side; and on the other, seriousness, forethought, modest courage, brotherliness, submission to God.

And this contrast gives a new character to the great central action of the play, the battle of Agincourt, which is now raised, . . . "from the historic level of a conflict between 'two mighty monarchies' to the epic height of a Divine decision and judgment. We are witnesses of something more than national prowess or personal achievement, however heroic,"—we witness the vindication by Divine Providence of that moral law in accordance with which wisdom prospers and folly perishes miserably.

And what has been the effect upon the audience of what they have seen? Surely in the first place a warm admiration for the hero King and his brave companions, and next a deepened sense of a Divine Power ruling the issues of righteousness.

And with these feelings has come a third. The men who, under God, won the battle of Agincourt were Englishmen, and the virtues they showed there were the characteristic virtues of the best Englishmen in all ages . . .

Feeling of this sort led to production of the play during World War 2, and still is influential. A recent editor calls the drama "the finest expression of English patriotism."

Of its center, Henry V himself, another critic says that

Shakespeare's efforts were mainly concentrated on the portraiture of 'this star of England,' Henry V, whom he deliberately chose out of the pages of history as the finest representative of the best distinctive type of English character ... Shakespeare has in no other play cast a man so entirely in the heroic mould as King Henry . . . On his virtues alone a full blaze of light is shed . . . Henry is his only male character who, when drawn at full length, betrays no crucial or invincible defect of will, or mind, or temper . . . Certainly no other of Shakespeare's monarchs is comparable with Henry V. In the rest of his English historical plays, he tells sad stories of the deaths of the kings, who are ruined mainly by moral flaws in their character. *Richard II, Richard III, King John,* even *Henry IV,* illustrate the unworthiness of those who thirst for kingly glory, the brittleness rather than the brilliance of the royal state. Only Henry V proves himself deserving of truly royal prosperity, of which the last scene of the play seems to guarantee him lasting enjoyment. Alone in Shakespeare's gallery of English monarchs does Henry's portrait evoke at once a joyous sense of satisfaction in the high potentialities of human character and a sense of pride among Englishmen that a man of his mettle is of English race.

This opinion today prevails; Henry V is Shakespeare's ideal king.

Yet there have been voices on the other side. William Hazlitt was outspoken:

Henry V is a very favorite monarch with the English nation, and he appears to have been also a favorite with Shakespeare, who labors hard to apologize for the actions of the king, by showing us the character of the man, as 'the king of good fellows.' He scarcely deserves this honour. He was fond of war and low company:— we know little else of him. He was careless, dissolute, and ambitious;— idle or doing mischief . . . In public affairs he seemed to have no idea of any rule of right or wrong, but brute force, glossed over with a little religious hypocrisy and arch-episcopal advice. His principles did not change with his situation and professions. His adventure on Gadshill was a prelude to the affair of Agincourt, only a bloodless one; Falstaff was a puny prompter of violence and outrage, compared with the pious and politic Archbishop of Canterbury, who gave the king *carte blanche,* in a genealogical tree of his family, to rob and murder in circles of latitude and longitude abroad—to save the possessions of the church at home. This appears in the speeches in Shakespeare, where the hidden motives that actuate princes and their advisers in war and policy are better laid open than in speeches from the throne or woolsack. Henry, because he did not know how to govern his own kingdom, determined to make war upon his neighbors. Because his own title to the crown was doubtful, he laid claim to that of France. Because he did not know how to exercise the enormous power, which had just dropped into his hands, to any one good purpose, he immediately undertook (a cheap and obvious resource of sovereignty) to do all the mischief he could . . . Henry declares his resolution 'when France is his, to bend it to his awe, or break it all to pieces'—a resolution worthy of a conqueror, to destroy all that he cannot enslave; and what adds to the joke, he lays all the blame of the consequences of his ambition on those who will not submit tamely to his tyranny. Such is the history of kingly power, from the beginning to the end of the world . . . Henry V, it is true, was a hero, a King of England, and the conqueror of the king of France. Yet we feel little love or admiration for him. He was a hero, that is, he was ready to sacrifice his own life for the pleasure of destroying thousands of other lives;—he was a conqueror of the French king, and for this we dislike him less than if he had conquered the French people. How then do we like him? We like him in.the play. There he is a very amiable monster, a very splendid pageant. As we like to gaze at a panther or a young lion in their cages in the Tower, and catch a pleasing horror from their glistening eyes, their velvet paws, and dreadless roar, so we take a very romantic, heroic, patriotic, and poetical delight in the boasts and feats of our younger Harry, as they appear on the stage and are confined to lines of ten syllables; where no blood follows the stroke that wounds our ears, where no harvest bends beneath horses' hoofs, no city flames, no little child is butchered, no dead men's bodies are found piled on heaps and festering the next morning—in the orchestra!

Hazlitt himself admits that he was writing politics, and that is evident, even though I have omitted the contemporary references. For that reason, there has been some dismissing of his criticism as written by the political radical rather than by the critic of drama. Yet there is dramatic criticism remaining, derived in part from Schlegel, who writes:

However much Shakespeare celebrates the French conquest of Henry, he still has not omitted to hint, after his way, the secret springs of this undertaking. Henry was in want of foreign war to secure himself on the throne; the clergy also wished to keep him employed abroad, and made an offer of rich contributions to prevent the passing of a law which would have deprived them of the half of their revenues. His learned bishops consequently are as ready to prove to him his indisputable right to the crown of France, as he is to allow his conscience to be tranquilized by them. They prove that the Salic law is not, and never was, applicable to France; and the matter is treated in a more succinct and convincing manner than such subjects usually are in manifestoes. After his renowned battles, Henry wished to secure his conquests by marriage with a French princess; all that has reference to this is intended for irony in the play. The fruit of this union, from which two nations promised to themselves such happiness in future, was the weak and feeble Henry VI, under whom everything was so miserably lost. It must not, therefore, be imagined that it was without the knowledge and will of the poet that a heroic drama turns out a comedy in his hands, and ends in the manner of comedy with a marriage of convenience.

In his translation of *Henry V,* Schlegel made some errors, such as interpreting the name of the elder tree, e-l-d-e-r, as meaning older. For the most part, however, he translated carefully, and that means that he read the text with care. So his criticism is written with knowledge of that whereof he speaks.

Others have spoken in the same vein. One thinks Henry's second speech before Harfleur, with its threats for the sacking of the town, "about the ugliest Shakespeare ever put into any mouth." Another calls it an "orgy of blood lust." Another asks: "What of King Henry's prayer in this play? Is the 'God of Battles' [whom Henry invokes] merely an Englishman's God, a tribal God?" The same sentiment appears in what is called "Henry's confusion of Mars with the Christian God."

When some interpret Shakespeare as presenting in Henry a character without defect, the Englishman's ideal king, and others are willing to call the campaign in France "an abominable piece of commercial militarism," by a "blood-stained king," "a temper-mad, prisoner-slaying savage," a further look at the play is in order.

The material of *Henry V* came from three places: (1) the old play of *The Famous Victories of Henry V;* (2) Holinshed and other historians; (3) Shakespeare's own stores. With the poet's language that gives this matter its force, I can here deal only by means of quotation.

The Famous Victories offered little to a dramatist already familiar with the type of dramatic plot that follows history like a pageant; in this instance the old plot is so summary that Shakespeare was obliged to use Holinshed as though there were not already a drama on the invasion of France. In the old play, however, he had before him the example of limiting the French wars to Agincourt, without all the succeeding battle and siege and diplomacy that the historian records. In one instance, *The Famous Victories* uses a historical bit not in Holinshed. The French are confident because their enemies are out of provisions:

> Why, take an Englishman out of his warm bed
> And his stale drink but one month,

And alas! what will become of him (13.54)?

In Shakespeare the idea appears thus:

Constable. Give them great meals of beef and iron and steel, they will eat like wolves and fight like devils.

Orleans. Ay, but these English are shrewdly out of beef (3.7.161).

Beef, however, is not mentioned in the old play, but does occur in Hall's *Chronicle.* Shakespeare's addition of iron and steel and his omission of beds and drink show his sense of effect. In *The Famous Victories,* as in *Henry V,* the insulting tennis balls are in a *tun* rather than in Holinshed's *barrel,* and likewise the plays put in the Dauphin's mouth a reference to Henry's wild youth, not so assigned in the *Chronicles* (2.4.28; 11.12).

The comedy of *The Famous Victories* is distributed throughout in roughly alternate scenes, as in *Henry V,* and its characters are cowardly soldiers; one scene has some suggestion of that in which Pistol captures a Frenchman. Above all, it provides the seed from which grew the comedy involving Princess Katharine and the King in Shakespeare's last scene. So when Shakespeare decided to close his play with this scene more than half comic, he developed a hint to be found in the workmanship of his humble predecessor. Not only the Princess and King Harry, but the Duke of Burgundy, another character from the serious action, is given an amusing part.

From Holinshed our author took much, dramatizing and expanding in his own poetic language and adding new matter.[1]

First of all, in the closely linked *Second Part of Henry IV,* that ruler, advising his son from his death-bed, speaks of certain friends

By whose fell working I was first advanced
And by whose power I well might lodge a fear
To be again displaced; which to avoid,
I cut them off; and had a purpose now
To lead out many to the Holy Land,
Lest rest and lying still might make them look
Too near unto my state. Therefore, my Harry,
Be it thy course to busy giddy minds
With foreign quarrels; that action, hence borne out,
May waste the memory of the former days (4.5.205).

From Holinshed comes this plan for an expedition to the Holy Land, but the reason for it and the conclusion that follows are added by Shakespeare from his stores of Machiavellian precept.

The Florentine Secretary knew that they who raise a usurper to power are likely soon to be his worst enemies. For their services they expect great

---

[1] Most of the material in Holinshed which Shakespeare uses may be found, in the order of the play, in W. G. Boswell-Stone, *Shakespeare's Holinshed* (London, 1896). In the Holinshed of 1587, it is found in 3.543-84; in that of 1808 in 3.57-134. I give references when using passages not found in Boswell-Stone.

rewards, greater than the new monarch can allow them. In their anger over thwarted expectations, they strive to overthrow him. The other matter of policy is that a ruler who feels insecure at home can with foreign wars divert his restless subjects from making trouble. It is true that these reasons for Henry's French invasion—having nothing to do with its justice—are not repeated in *Henry V* itself. The reason is dramatic; the drama opens not at the beginning of the action but plunges into the midst of things. As Lancaster says at the end of *Henry IV*, the King is already "pleased" with the notion of carrying sword and fire into France. Since at the opening of *Henry V* he has already pressed his claim to the French crown, and the French ambassadors with a reply have actually come to England, the appropriate time for dealing with underlying motives has passed by. So closely connected with this play is the preceding one that its presentation of motive may be assumed as not impertinent.

From Holinshed comes the primary material of the first act. The clergy, fearing that much of their property will be taken over by the nation, make an attempt, similar in motive to that advised by the dying Henry IV, to divert attention from their wealth by a foreign war. Their plan, as he fits it to the stage, Shakespeare puts in the Archbishop's mouth, thereby obliging himself to modify Holinshed's comment that the wealth of the Church had been "devoutly given, and disordinately spent by religious and other spiritual persons." Though the dramatist's Canterbury says the property has been given by "men devout," he naturally omits that he and his fellow clerics have spent its returns improperly. Holinshed lays the onus of suggesting the war on the Archbishop; Shakespeare retains a hint of this in making the Archbishop say:

> I have made an offer . . .
> In regard of causes now in hand,
> Which I have opened to his grace at large,
> As touching France, to give a greater sum (1.1.75).

But the playwright, since he chose to begin his action after the King has asserted his claim, is led to make Henry ask the Archbishop's advice, to be given "justly and religiously" as counsel "in your conscience washed as pure as sin with baptism" (1.2.31)—something that Holinshed suggests only in concluding his account of this reign, where the monarch says:

> Before the beginning of the same wars, he was fully persuaded by men both wise and of great holiness of life that upon such intent he might and ought both begin the same wars and follow them till he had brought them to an end justly and rightly, and that without all danger of God's displeasure or peril of soul.[2]

---

2 Ed. of 1587: 3.583 ; ed. of 1808: 3.133.

In the playwright's hands this becomes:

> For God doth know how many now in health
> Shall drop their blood in approbation
> Of what your reverence shall incite us to.
> Therefore take heed how you impawn our person,
> How you awake our sleeping sword of war:
> We charge you in the name of God, take heed;
> For never two such kingdoms did contend
> Without much fall of blood; whose guiltless drops
> Are every one a woe, a sore complaint
> 'Gainst him whose wrongs give edge unto the swords
> That make such waste in brief mortality (1.2.18).

In Holinshed there are at this point no such sentiments. When later they occur, they are brief and formal. The historian's Archbishop in his attempt to save the Church's property exhorts Henry

> to advance forth his banner to fight for his right, to conquer his inheritance, to spare neither blood, sword, nor fire; sith his war was just, his cause good, and his claim true.

This also supports anxious inquiries about justice by Shakespeare's king, and underlies bloody speeches by his Archbishop, urging Henry

> With blood and sword and fire to win your right (1.2.131).

Both the *Chronicles* and *The Famous Victories* show that if France is to be invaded, preparations must be made to defend England against the Scotch. Shakespeare followed the former, since the couplet

> If that you will France win,
> Then with Scotland first begin (1.2.167)

appears in that order in Holinshed, but in the old play is

> He that will Scotland win,
> Must first with France begin (9.88)

One Shakespearean addition at this point was calculated to win applause in the time before James VI became James I:

> Once the eagle England being in prey,
> To her unguarded nest the weasel Scot
> Comes sneaking and so sucks her princely eggs,
> Playing the mouse in absence of the cat,
> To tear and havoc more than she can eat (1.2.169).

England is a bird of prey, though a noble one; Scotland an ignoble animal, one of "the petty thieves." Whether it is patriotism to make England an eagle, or whether our dramatist is comparing two thievish creatures may be debated. There is no suggestion that either England or Scotland have in their attacks on one another the justice that Henry eagerly seeks in order to make bloodshed in France righteous. Meditating on defense, Exeter says:

> While that the armed hand doth fight abroad
> The advised head defends itself at home,
> For government, though high and low and lower,
> Put into parts, doth keep in one consent,
> Congreeing in a full and natural close,
> Like music (1.2.178).

What is essentially the continuation of this speech is given to Canterbury:

> Therefore doth heaven divide
> The state of man in divers functions,
> Setting endeavor in continual motion,
> To which is fixed, as an aim or butt,
> Obedience; for so work the honey-bees,
> Creatures that by a rule in nature teach
> The act of order to a peopled kingdom.
> They have a king and officers of sorts,
> Where some, like magistrates, correct at home;
> Others, like merchants, venture trade abroad;
> Others, like soldiers, armed in their stings,
> Make boot upon the summer's velvet buds,
> Which pillage they with merry march bring home
> To the tent-royal of their emperor,
> Who, busied in his majesty, surveys
> The singing masons building roofs of gold,
> The civil citizens kneading up the honey,
> The poor mechanic porters crowding in
> Their heavy burdens at his narrow gate,
> The sad-eyed justice, with his surly hum,
> Delivering o'er to executors pale
> The lazy yawning drone. I this infer,
> That many things, having full reference
> To one consent, may work contrariously,
> As many arrows, loosed several ways,
> Come to one mark; as many ways meet in one town;
> As many fresh streams meet in one salt sea;
> As many lines close in the dial's center;
> So may a thousand actions, once afoot,
> End in one purpose, and be all well borne
> Without defeat (1.2.183).

Shakespeare then shifts abruptly to the French expedition, covered by saying that only one quarter of England is to be taken to France. In truth, however, there is no close connection between preparing for the French campaign and the functions of the citizens in a well-regulated state. Henry's concern is with immediate conflict, not war's economic background. The passage suggests others in Shakespeare. One is the comic fable of the belly and the members in *Coriolanus* (1.1). In the second, Ulysses, touching, like Canterbury, on the figure of the beehive, but otherwise making his rhetoric more splendid, talks on "specialty of rule," and on "degree," in *Troilus and Cressida* (1.3). The three passages suggest that the idea of divided function in the well-ordered state was one that continued long in Shakespeare's mind, and on which he was pleased to speak, even when, as in *Henry V,* his plot offered but slight opportunity.

Shakespeare then puts in Henry's mouth a stern resolution:

> By God's help,
> And yours, the noble sinews of our power,
> France being ours, we'll bend it to our awe
> Or break it all to pieces: or there we'll sit,
> Ruling in large and ample empery
> O'er France and all her almost kingly dukedoms,
> Or lay these bones in an unworthy urn (1.2.222).

Here meet religion and an ambition that disregards the happiness of both conqueror and conquered in the spirit of rule or ruin.

Shakespeare next conflates two French embassies, that of the tennis balls and a later one, and Henry's replies to both. The Chronicler gives his second answer thus:

> I little esteem your French brags, and set less by your power and strength; I know perfectly my right to my region, which you usurp; and except you deny the apparent truth, so do yourselves also; if you neither do nor will know it, yet God and the world knoweth it. The power of your master you see, but my puissance ye have not yet tasted. If he have loving subjects, I am (I thank God) not unstored of the same; and I say this unto you, that before one year pass, I trust to make the highest crown of your country to stoop, and the proudest miter to learn his humiliation. In the mean time tell this to the usurper your master, that within three months I will enter into France as mine own true and lawful patrimony, appointing to acquire the same not with brag of words, but with deeds of men and dint of sword, by the aid of God, in whom is my whole trust and confidence.[3]

The spirit of this appears variously throughout the play, as when Henry assures Katharine that he is not a man of words (5.2.137); it is plainest in his reply to the ambassador:

---

3 1587: 3.547-8; 1808: 3.69.

> We never valued this poor seat of England; . . .
> But tell the Dauphin I will keep my state,
> Be like a king and show my sail of greatness
> When I do rouse me in my throne of France . . .
>   I will rise there with so full a glory
> That I will dazzle all the eyes of France,
> Yea, strike the Dauphin blind to look on us.
> And tell the pleasant prince this mock of his
> Hath turned his balls to gun-stones; and his soul
> Shall stand sore-charged for the wasteful vengeance
> That shall fly with them; for many a thousand widows
> Shall this his mock mock out of their dear husbands;
> Mock mothers from their sons, mock castles down;
> And some are yet ungotten and unborn
> That shall have cause to curse the Dauphin's scorn.
> But this lies all within the will of God,
> To whom I do appeal; and in whose name
> Tell you the Dauphin I am coming on,
> To venge me as I may and to put forth
> My rightful hand in a well-hallowed cause (1.2.269).

Shakespeare, starting from the Chronicler's "Paris balls" and "London balls," intensified the horrors of war, and gave emphasis to the responsibility for them of French royalty; Henry's appeal to God and justice, as reported by the Historian, was hardly to be heightened. The King's depreciation of "this poor seat of England" is in harmony neither with historical expression of trust in his subjects, nor with the patriotism of the drama itself. By the words *valued* and *poor,* we are led to remember "the almost kingly dukedoms" that Henry hopes to control in rich France, and to anticipate the "petty and unprofitable dukedoms" he is to reject, as though England, where he is "from home," served only as a basis for ambition rather than as a land where duty required him "to maintain the peace."

At any rate, the Chorus beginning the second act is again patriotic:

> O England! model to thy inward greatness
> Like little body with a mighty heart,

though profit appears as well:

> Now sits Expectation in the air
> And hides a sword from hilts unto the point
> With crowns imperial, crowns and coronets,
> Promised to Henry and his followers.

In this second act is the conspiracy by the Earl of Cambridge and others, only slightly related to the campaign in France which is the central action of the drama. Indeed if the scene were omitted, it would leave no trace. The author of *The Famous Victories* ignores it. The King's plan for making the conspirators deprive themselves of mercy by demanding severe punishment for a similar offender is not in the *Chronicles;* yet aside from it, the material of the conspiracy is found there. Was Shakespeare so preoccupied with history that he was unwilling to omit any important event that fell within the time limits of his play? That he paused for it indicates that he was not thinking in terms of a unified dramatic action. Yet the scene has dramatic quality, as when the traitors, suddenly realizing they are caught, are overcome with terror. Henry's address to the conspirators, the longest speech in this play in which the hero several times speaks at length, has quality which must have made it tremendous as an oration on the Elizabethan stage. The conspiracy, though presented only for itself, and little related to the remainder of the drama, does strengthen the king with spectators who see him endangered by unprovoked treachery.

The conclusion of this scene reaffirms ideas already made prominent, but not at this point in Holinshed; divine aid, and success or utter ruin:

> Let us deliver
> Our puissance into the hand of God
> Putting it straight in expedition.
> Cheerly to sea! the signs of war advance:
> No king of England, if not king of France (2.2.189).

From the *Chronicles* come the negotiations with the French to which the last scene of Act 2 is devoted. Henry informs King Charles that the latter is holding his throne contrary to the laws of God and man, and that by his perversity in refusing to yield, he forces the English to take arms. Through his ambassador, Henry exhorts Charles "in the bowels of Jesu Christ to render him that which was his own; whereby effusion of Christian blood might be avoided." The poet expands the trite diplomatic or military phrasing to a concrete and moving pronouncement on the horrors of war:

> He wills you, in the name of God Almighty,
> That you divest yourself, and lay apart
> The borrowed glories that by gift of Heaven,
> By law of nature and of nations, 'long
> To him and to his heirs . . .
> And bids you, in the bowels of the Lord,
> Deliver up the crown, and to take mercy
> On the poor souls for whom this hungry war
> Opens his vasty jaws; and on your head
> Turning the widows' tears, the orphans' cries,

> The dead men's blood, the pining maidens' groans,
> For husbands, fathers, and betrothed lovers,
> That shall be swallowed in this controversy (2.4.77).

However much Shakespeare expands, he has his base in the *Chronicles,* where the French monarch, refusing to surrender his hereditary throne, is thereby made responsible for the English invasion. Shakespeare not only retains this blame, but has Exeter, dropping assertion of justice, make a further threat of war in revenge for the personal insult to Henry in the mock of the tennis balls.

Much of this second act is given to the comic characters substituted for those of *The Famous Victories.* They, like Henry and his nobles, have their financial expectations from France. Pistol declares

> I shall sutler be
> Unto the camp, and profits will accrue (2.1.114).

Still more directly he reveals how, while the aristocracy are getting their "crowns and coronets," he and his comrades will fulfill their hopes:

> Yoke-fellows in arms,
> Let us to France; like horse-leeches, my boys,
> To suck, to suck, the very blood to suck (2.3.53).

As the Chronicler continues, he relates that King Charles offered "to the King of England a great sum of money, with divers countries, being in very deed but base and poor, as a dowery with the Lady Katharine in marriage." In the chorus beginning Act 3, Shakespeare makes the offer to the invader of these "petty and unprofitable dukedoms," insufficient to break off his attack on Harfleur. The attack itself, recounted briefly by the historian, is freely expanded by Shakespeare, somewhat in the tone of Holinshed's earlier narrative of the siege of Rouen, where Henry declares his ability to destroy the people with "blood, fire, and famine." First comes the speech beginning:

> Once more unto the breach, dear friends, once more;
> Or close the wall up with our English dead!

and he urges them to be tigers, to

> Disguise fair nature with hard-favored rage;
> . . .   and upon this charge
> Cry "God for Harry! England and Saint George!" (3.1)

The comic scene immediately following is a parody of its predecessor:

> *Bardolph.* On, on, on, on, on! to the breach, to the breach!
> *Nym.* Pray thee, corporal, stay: the knocks are too hot; and for mine own part, I have not a case of lives . . .
> *Pistol.* Knocks go and come: God's vassals drop and die;
>   And sword and shield

> In bloody field
> Doth win immortal fame.

Boy. Would I were in an alehouse in London! I would give all my
fame for a pot of ale, and safety . . .

Fluellen. Up to the breach, you dogs! Avaunt, you cullions!

And still another variation from Macmorris:

> The town is beseeched, and the trumpet calls us to the breach; and
> we talk and be Chrish, do nothing; 'tis shame for us all; so God sa' me,
> 'tis shame to stand still; it is shame, by my hand; and there is throats
> to be cut, and works to be done (3.2.107).

The next scene opens with the exhortation by which Henry frightens the
citizens of Harfleur into surrender:

> This is the latest parle we will admit.
> Therefore to our best mercy give yourselves;
> Or like to men proud of destruction
> Defy us to our worst; for as I am a soldier,
> A name that in my thoughts becomes me best,
> If I begin the battery once again,
> I will not leave the half-achieved Harfleur
> Till in her ashes she lie buried.
> The gates of mercy shall be all shut up,
> And the fleshd soldier, rough and hard of heart,
> In liberty of bloody hand shall range
> With conscience wide as hell, mowing like grass
> Your fresh-fair virgins and your flowering infants.
> What is it then to me, if impious war,
> Arrayd in flames like to the prince of fiends,
> Do, with his smirchd complexion, all fell feats
> Enlinkd to waste and desolation?
> What is't to me, when you yourselves are cause,
> If your pure maidens fall into the hand
> Of hot and forcing violation?
> What rein can hold licentious wickedness
> When down the hill he holds his fierce career?
> We may as bootless spend our vain command
> Upon the enraged soldiers in their spoil
> As send precepts to the leviathan
> To come ashore. Therefore, you men of Harfleur,
> Take pity of your town and of your people,
> Whiles yet my soldiers are in my command;
> Whiles yet the cool and temperate wind of grace

> O'erblows the filthy and contagious clouds
> Of heady murder, spoil and villany.
> If not, why in a moment, look to see
> The blind and bloody soldier with foul hand
> Defile the locks of your shrill-shrieking daughters;
> Your fathers taken by the silver beards,
> And their most reverend heads dashd to the walls;
> Your naked infants spitted upon pikes,
> Whiles the mad mothers with their howls confusd
> Do break the clouds, as did the wives of Jewry
> At Herod's bloody-hunting slaughtermen.
> What say you? will you yield, and this avoid?
> Or, guilty in defence, be thus destroyed? (3.3.2)

This terrible speech, depending on no more than Holinshed's statement that "the town was sacked, to the great gain of the Englishmen," is perhaps the most elaborate presentation by any great poet of the horrors war brings on an innocent people. If Shakespeare got hints from Harington's *Orlando Furioso* (40.30-32), he has gone beyond his original. The passage fits with the play's lesser speeches on military destruction, and in its central position does much toward setting the tone of the whole. Here as elsewhere, Henry lays all the blame on his adversaries. The governor of the city answers as though he had not been listening to such savage threats:

> Great King,
> We yield our town and lives to thy soft mercy.

This is the reply to a softer speech than Henry's. Can we infer that the royal savagery is an afterthought, replacing words less terrible? Shakespeare then has the King command: "Use mercy to them all." Yet Holinshed reports that

> Some writing of this yielding up of Harfleur do in like sort mention of the distress whereto the people, then expelled out of their habitations, were driven; inasmuch as parents with their children, young maids, and old folk went out of the town gates with heavy hearts (God wot) as put to their present shifts to seek them a new abode (1587: 3.550; 1808: 73-4.)

Their places were supplied with English immigrants. If we believe with Machiavelli that such methods are utterly cruel, opposed not merely to what is Christian but what is human (*Discourses* 1.26), this action blackens the victor's character.

After Henry's horrible threats, if ever the notion of comic relief is to be invoked, this is the time for it. Princess Katharine's lesson in English follows. This seems wholly of Shakespeare's devising. Its comedy is heightened by infusion of bawdry, repeated often enough to make sure that the audience get it, with the *foot* and the *count*. The bad quarto spells *con. Coun,* the reading of modern texts, is without textual authority.

Shakespeare next follows the Historian with a council by the French, in which they arrogantly plan to bring the captive king of England into Rouen in a chariot (3.5.54). Shakespeare also represents them as reckoning on the ransom of the invader, something not mentioned until later by the *Chronicles.*

Even the comic plot shows dependence on Holinshed, in the service at the bridge lauded by Fluellen, and the theft by Bardolph of a "pax of little price" (3.6.47), for which he is hanged. Into the form of orders by the King, Shakespeare puts Holinshed's assertion that nothing was taken from the country-people without payment (3.6.110).

In expanding the account of King Henry's answer to the French herald, Shakespeare retains from the *Chronicles* the poetical words:

> We shall your tawnie ground with your red blood
> Discolour (3.6.162).

In both history and play, Henry's speeches in this context are full of his dependence on God.

In the next scene the overconfident French nobles indulge in bawdy jesting. Shakespeare founds this on Holinshed's account of their throwing dice for the prisoners they expect to take; the actual dicing the dramatist glances at here (3.7.95) and reaffirms in the Prologue to Act 4.

Entirely of Shakespeare's devising is Henry's conversation, in disguise, with some of his soldiers. When he asserts his own courage, Bates replies:

> I would he were here alone; so should he be sure to be
> ransomed, and a many poor men's lives saved (4.1.123).

Henry answers:

> Methinks I could not die anywhere so contented as in the
> King's company, his cause being just and his quarrel
> honorable.

Williams does not admit this as certain, and continues with a variation on the theme of war's frightfulness:

> If the cause be not good, the King himself hath a heavy reckoning to make; when all those legs and arms and heads, chopped off in a battle, shall join together at the latter day, and cry all, "We died at such a place," some swearing, some crying for a surgeon, some upon wives left poor behind them, some upon the debts they owe, some upon their children rawly left. I am afeard there are few die well that die in a battle; for how can they charitably dispose of anything when blood is their argument? Now, if these men do not die

well, it will be a black matter for the King that led them to it; whom
to disobey were against all proportion of subjection (4.1.140).

Williams here passes beyond the question of righteous war to the wick-
edness that all war carries with it. At least, if he intends any qualification
to "I am afeard there are few die well that die in a battle," he does not
express it. But even the question of just war, on which Henry had been so
careful to question the Archbishop, he here evades, turning from the monarch's responsibility when he wages war, just or unjust, to the soldier's
individual morality; war, he declares, is God's beadle, God's vengeance,
concluding:

> Every soldier in the wars [should] do as every sick
> man in his bed, wash every mote out of his conscience;
> and dying so, death is to him advantage; or not dying,
> the time was blessedly lost wherein such preparation was
> gained: and in him that escapes, it were not sin to think
> that, making God so free an offer, He let him outlive
> that day to see His greatness, and to teach others how
> they should prepare (4.1.178).

So the warlike King is a benefactor to the men whose bodies are to wall
up the breaches made in foreign ramparts.

When after some quarreling the soldiers move off, Henry meditates on
the monarch's sufferings for the sake of his people:

> Upon the king! let us our lives, our souls,
> Our debts, our careful wives,
> Our children and our sins lay on the king!
> We must bear all. O hard condition,
> Twin-born with greatness, subject to the breath
> Of every fool, whose sense no more can feel
> But his own wringing! What infinite heart's ease
> Must kings neglect, that private men enjoy!
> And what have kings that privates have not too,
> Save ceremony, save general ceremony?
> And what are thou, thou idol ceremony?
> What kind of god art thou, that suffer'st more
> Of mortal griefs than do thy worshippers?
> What are thy rents? what are thy comings in?
> O ceremony, show me but thy worth!
> What is thy soul of adoration?
> Art thou aught else but place, degree, and form,
> Creating awe and fear in other men?
> Wherein thou art less happy being fear'd

Than they in fearing.
What drink'st thou oft, instead of homage sweet,
But poison'd flattery? O, be sick, great greatness,
And bid thy ceremony give thee cure!
Think'st thou the fiery fever will go out
With titles blown from adulation?
Will it give place to flexure and low bending?
Canst thou, when thou command'st the begger's knee,
Command the health of it? No, thou proud dream,
That play'st so subtly with a king's repose,
I am a king that find thee, and I know
'Tis not the balm, the scepter, and the ball,
The sword, the mace, the crown imperial,
The intertissued robe of gold and pearl,
The farced title running 'fore the king,
The throne he sits on, nor the tide of pomp
That beats upon the high shore of this world,
No, not all these, thrice-gorgeous ceremony,
Not all these, laid in bed majestical,
Can sleep so soundly as the wretched slave,
Who with a body fill'd and vacant mind
Gets him to rest, cramm'd with distressful bread;
Never sees horrid night, the child of hell,
But like a lackey, from the rise to set
Sweats in the eye of Phoebus, and all night
Sleeps in Elysium. Next day, after dawn,
Doth rise and help Hyperion to his horse,
And follows so the ever-running year,
With profitable labor, to his grave.
And but for ceremony, such a wretch,
Winding up days with toil and nights with sleep,
Had the forehand and vantage of a king.
The slave, a member of the country's peace,
Enjoys it; but in gross brain little wots
What watch the king keeps to maintain the peace
Whose hours the peasant best advantages (4.1.246).

This theme of the vexations of the ruler, de infelicitatibus principum as
Poggio Bracciolini called it, had already engaged Shakespeare in *Richard
II* (4.1.194); indeed much of the play exemplifies it. In the second part of
Henry IV are the lines on the "polish'd perturbation, golden care"
(4.5.23). The present soliloquy is justified in its position by the remarks

of the soldiers, but it does not deal with military affairs and with the troubles of the soldier king; indeed it is applied to the monarch who preserves peace for his peasantry rather than to one who leads them to conquest. It is, then, essentially intrusive, saying not what the plot demands but what the dramatist had ready in his own mind, and therefore let his king say, with such eloquence.

Immediately comes further emphasis on the King's piety, of a sort not here suggested by Holinshed. Henry calls on the "God of battles" (4.1.306) to steel his soldier's hearts, and then prays that the Lord will not punish him for his father's guilt in King Richard's death, for which he has attempted to atone by offerings to charity and religion. Victory in his eyes is at that moment a reward for personal piety, without regard to the justice of his cause.

The outline of the military, as distinguished from the comic part of Agincourt, is from the *Chronicles*. Holinshed tells of a "right grave oration" in which Henry harangued his soldiers, "moving them to play the men, whereby to obtain a glorious victory."[4] The speech on Saint Crispin's day, though not a formal address, is its substitute, spoken before the "hoast" though beginning as conversation with Westmoreland. Henry makes no reference to the justice of his cause, but declares:

> If it be a sin to covet honor,
> I am the most offending soul alive (4.3.28).

Honor seems here the "vain renown and worldly fame," which Holinshed says that on his deathbed the King disclaimed.[5] At any rate, honor, not his just right, now explains the king's desire to fight. In his speech, too, gathering "brothers, friends, and countrymen" from the preceding chorus, Henry gives the chief basis for admiring his equalitarianism:

> We few, we happy few, we band of brothers;
> For he today that sheds his blood with me
> Shall be my brother; be he ne'er so vile,
> This day shall gentle his condition (4.3.60).

Whether the King shed any blood in the battle, neither Holinshed nor Shakespeare informs us, nor does the dramatist tell us whether Williams the soldier did. At any rate the latter is the subject of a "rather crude jest of the King's," when he is led to challenge the glove that Henry "by bargain" should wear himself. Moreover the King so harshly accuses the soldier of abusing him that proper is the comment: "The situation is saved by [the] manly words of the common soldier." The Monarch's response to them is:

> Here, uncle Exeter, fill this glove with crowns,

---

4 1587: 3.553; 1808: 3.79.
5 See p. 63, below.

And give it to this fellow. Keep it, fellow;
And wear it for an honor in thy cap
Till I do challenge it. Give him the crowns (4.8.61).
Any part Williams took in the battle did not "gentle his condition;" when
the King calls him "fellow," he is so far from meaning "brother" that
the word emphasizes the difference between them. How much connection is
there here between word and act? Is the offer of brotherhood by making the
vilest gentle, not by admitting common humanity, such a speech as men
of position make, with induced sincerity, when they wish popular support?
Is the jest a proper prank for a man of exalted station, to be justified by
his condescending largess of a glove full of coins? If Shakespeare is a
painstaking artist, the comedy of this play is related to its history, and the
King's character is compounded of all he says and does.

Soon after the Monarch's equalitarian speech, the French herald appears
with an offer of ransom. This Henry has already disclaimed to Bates
and Williams, and now again he declares for death rather than surrender.
To the *Chronicles* the play adds reminders of the horrors of war: Mountjoy
speaks of festering corpses, and Henry himself of Englishmen's bodies
buried in dunghills (4.3.87,101). Pistol's comedy, coming directly after,
echoes this with cutting throats and sucking blood (4.4.33,66). Still
further, when Mountjoy asks to be allowed to bury the French dead after
the battle, he describes the field, where

Many of our princes—woe the while!—

Lie drowned and soaked in mercenary blood;
So do our vugar drench their peasant limbs
In blood of princes; and their wounded steeds
Fret fetlock-deep in gore, and with wild rage
Yerk out their armed heels at their dead masters,
Killing them twice (4.7.73).

In drawing from Holinshed the casualty roll of the battle, Shakespeare
represents the English slain as four men of rank and but twenty-five
others. Holinshed does give that number as reported by some, but adds that
other writers of greater credit affirm that the number was above five or
six hundred.

After the battle, as a recent writer puts it, "Shakespeare's Henry V
out-Henries the historical Henry in his recognition of his dependence upon
God as the giver of victory. At times his references to God seem a little
out of place in the context." With one of these references, Henry, on win-
ning the victory, commands:

Be it death proclaimed through our host,
To boast of this or take the praise from God,

Which is his only (4.8.119).

When Fluellen asks: "Is it not lawful, an please Your Majesty, to tell how many is killed?" He is answered; "Yes, Captain; but with this acknowledgement, that God fought for us." The comic Welshman retorts: "Yes, my conscience, he did us great good." Without heeding, the King goes on to historical directions for public thanksgiving. But if Shakespeare did not intend Fluellen's unconvinced assent to be devastating to the victor's piety, why did he write it?

To the activity in bringing about a treaty of peace that the historical Duke of Burgundy engages in, Shakespeare adds a speech on the desolation of France by war:

        Let it not disgrace me
If I demand before this royal view
What rub or what impediment there is,
Why that the naked, poor, and mangled Peace,
Dear nurse of arts, plenties, and joyful births,
Should not in this best garden of the world
Our fertile France, put up her lovely visage?
Alas! She hath from France too long been chased,
And all her husbandry doth lie on heaps,
Corrupting in its own fertility.
Her vine, the merry cheerer of the heart,
Unpruned dies; her hedges even-pleach'd,
Like prisoners wildly overgrown with hair,
Put forth disordered twigs; her fallow leas
The darnel, hemlock, and rank fumitory
Doth root upon, while that the coulter rusts
That should deracinate such savagery;
The even mead, that erst brought sweetly forth
The freckled cowslip, burnet, and green clover,
Wanting the scythe, all uncorrected, rank,
Conceives by idleness, and nothing teems
But hateful docks, rough thistles, kecksies, burs,
Losing both beauty and utility;
And as our vineyards, fallows, meads, and hedges,
Defective in their natures, grow to wildness,
Even so our houses and ourselves and children
Have lost, or do not learn for want of time,
The sciences that should become our country,
But grow like savages—as soldiers will,
That nothing do but meditate on blood—

> To swearing and stern looks, diffused attire,
> And everything that seems unnatural.
> Which to reduce into our former favour
> You are assembled; and my speech entreats
> That I may know the let why gentle Peace
> Should not expel these inconveniences,
> And bless us with her former qualities (5.2.31).

This speech gives not only the effect of war on the country, but the effect of the military life on the soldier—another aspect of what Williams had striven to say in telling how men die in battle. Is Burgundy, when he makes the soldier a savage, reminding the reader of Henry's assertion when threatening Harfleur that in his thoughts the name of soldier becomes him best? At least Henry shows no humane appreciation of peace; unless he has his price, he is ready with more savagery:

> If, Duke of Burgundy, you would the peace,
> Whose want gives growth to the imperfections
> Which you have cited, you must buy that peace
> With full accord of all our just demands.

This answer is not in harmony with Holinshed's statement that the English king inclined to give terms because he did not wish to be considered "a causer of Christian blood still to be spent in his quarrel." About that, Shakespeare's monarch thinks little after his first long address to his Archbishop. The Historian also says that Henry minded "not to be reputed for a destroyer of [France], which he coveted to preserve"—to preserve, as Shakespeare early had him indicate, only if he could receive income from her. This desire now appears in Henry's "I love France so well that I will not part with a village of it; I will have it all mine," and his further admission in the same context that his wooing of Princess Katharine depends on covetousness for French territory:

> I am content [that Kate be my wife]; so the maiden cities you talk of
> may wait on her; so the maid that stood in the way for my wish shall
> show me the way to my will (5.2.353).

In the play's final scene, important negotiations for peace are mingled with unhistorical comedy by King Henry and Princess Katharine, who thus continue earlier roles. The grave Duke of Burgundy, speaking of Henry and the Princess, contributes Shakespearean bawdry in the tone of Mercutio:

> If you would conjure in her you must make a circle; if conjure up
> Love in her in his true likeness, he must appear naked and blind. Can
> you blame her then, being a maid yet rosed over with the virgin
> crimson of modesty, if she deny the appearance of a naked blind boy

in her naked seeing self? It were, my Lord, a hard condition for a maid to consign to.

King Henry. Yet they do wink and yield, as love is blind and enforces.

Burgundy. They are then excused, my lord, when they see not what they do.

King Henry. Then, good my lord, teach your cousin to consent winking.

Burgundy. I will wink on her to consent, my lord, if you will teach her to know my meaning; for maids, well summered and warm kept, are like flies at Bartholomew-tide, blind, though they have their eyes; and then they will endure handling, which before would not abide looking on.

King Henry. This moral ties me over to time and a hot summer; and so I shall catch the fly, your cousin, in the latter end, and she must be blind too (5.2.319).

and the play ends on a light note mingled with the serious:

Then shall I swear to Kate, and you to me;

And may our oaths well kept and prosperous be!

The bawdy comedy of this scene—Shakespeare's deliberate doing—reminds one of the close of a London marriage comedy by Middleton. It is hardly the proper conclusion for a play of dignified heroism. Especially as the last of so many comic scenes, what effect does it have on the total impression reader or spectator carries away, or should carry away, from the play?

With comedy, irony is mingled, as when the King says:

If ever thou be'st mine, Kate, . . . I get thee with scambling, and thou must therefore needs prove a good soldier-breeder. Shall not thou and I, between Saint Denis and Saint George, compound a boy, half French, half English, that shall go to Constantinople and take the Turk by the beard (5.2.215)?

This irony is reinforced in the serious part of the scene, when French king and queen predict that "never" shall there be war between England and France. In the Epilogue, referring to the plays on Henry VI, Shakespeare indicates that the boy compounded by King and Princess was so far from assailing the Turk that he could not keep England in order, much less retain France.

Varied, then, are the components of this complex play. Of the comedy that occupies one-third of it, part is given to characters who appear also in dignified roles. Part goes to those who exist only for comedy. These are at times virtually independent of the main action, as is Fluellen when he caricatures the learned soldier. At other times they parody the King's words, as when Pistol talks of cutting throats or Bardolph exhorts his companies to enter the breach. Above all, the King himself, when comic, comments on his own attitude as conqueror. If there is to be any thought of the effect of this play as a totality, its comedy necessarily—if only because of its bulk—receives much attention, much more than it commonly has been allowed.

The serious matter, in its patriotic glorification of King Henry, suggests the tone of Holinshed's final pages of eulogy, where the monarch in all his royal virtues is described as "a pattern in princehood, a lode-star in honor, and mirror of magnificence;" Shakespeare makes him "the mirror of all Christian kings," and "this star of England" (2, Chorus; final chorus). To put Holinshed on the stage required much modification, with always the possibility of different emphasis. A suspicious reader will wonder if Shakespeare intended to lower the value of Holinshed's praise of the king by putting it in the mouth of the selfish Archbishop of scene 1, but at least the Chronicler's seldom-abandoned tone of admiration is preserved.

Yet there are other passages in which Holinshed is so modified that the effect is quite different. Notable here is the play's emphasis on Henry's piety. He refers to God some thirty-five times, far oftener than any other Shakespearean character. Not only is the number increased over that of Holinshed, but there is a change from a ritualistic to a personal tone. Shakespeare is doing something with the King's piety that his source does not warrant.

The Chronicler's slight references to the horrors of war bear little relation to Shakespeare's, with their eloquent expansion. Their number and development and their support by the comedy make them important in the play, the most striking of Shakespeare's contributions as he turned history into drama. However we explain their relation to the whole, Shakespeare's interest in developing the theme of military bloodshed and ruin is evident.

Then there are the passages on the functions of various citizens and on the weary labors of the king, representing concern with political problems foreign to the play as hero-tale. They almost contradict the military story dealing with the citizen only as soldier, and exalting a warlike king little concerned with the normal distresses of the ruler.

How are all these elements to be related? Are we, going further even than Hazlitt, to interpret the work as a satire on a hypocrite whose ambition disregards the misery he causes? The sixteenth century knew ambition. Machiavelli wrote a poem on the subject in which he shows how it caused in the region of Verona such horrors of war as Henry threatened to Harfleur. Erasmus, in his *Institution of a Christian Prince,* spoke for peace and against slaughter-bringing ambition. Peace wearing her wheaten garland is in *Hamlet* Shakespeare's familiar allegory, summing up Burgundy's speech on France desolated. Holinshed indeed makes the King, not undisturbed by such thoughts, protest to those who surround his death-bed

> that neither the ambitious desire to enlarge his dominions, neither to purchase vain renown and worldly fame, nor any other consideration had moved him to take the wars in hand (1587: 3.583; 1808:3.132),

but only his desire to secure "a perfect peace, and come to enjoy those pieces of his inheritance which to him of right belonged." This is not the king who revenges the mock of the "Paris balls," who is proud to admit the sin of coveting honor. Indeed what consistency is there between refusal to enlarge dominions, and fighting to regain an inheritance of almost kingly dukedoms, some of which were abjured in the Black Prince's time? But the dramatist involves his hero in no such difficulty; Henry in the play, when once assured by the Archbishop, has no doubts of his own rectitude. Yet throughout the drama such doubt is suggested to the reader by emphasis on war's desolation.

The condition presented, in fact, is an anticipation of that in Thomas Hardy's *Dynasts,* where he recognizes the ability in battle and negotiation of his characters. Then he gives his own comments through the Spirit of the Pities or the Spirit Ironic. So Henry V shows his ability as a soldier, and yet, sometimes in his own words, sometimes in those of another, there comes implied comment pitiable or ironic. We hardly need attempt to break through Shakespeare's impartiality to ask whether he, like Hardy, is writing to the rebuke of man's folly. Yet to think the dramatist unconscious of what he was doing is not reasonable. He could not emphasize what the conqueror's ambition for fame and rich dominions did to his victims without seeing that the conqueror himself was not the perfection of human character, not the mirror of all Christian kings. Yet Anglo-Saxon patriotism, whether of Islanders or Anglophiles, has not been wholly wrong in supposing Henry to foreshadow the bearer of the white man's burden. Within the field of vision open to Holinshed and the author of *The Famous Victories,* Henry is a most satisfactory hero, aristrocratic yet able to meet the common man, brave, vigorous, successful. As the Peninsular soldier said of the Iron Duke, he "whops the Frenchies." With such a strong man in command, the morality of a war is easily forgotten. Though an empire stretching from Inverness to the Pyrenees was a monstrosity that never brought good to Henry II or any of his successors, much less to their insular or continental subjects, the Black Prince bears a glorious name.

Shakespeare, however, was accustomed to taking men as they are. He held the mirror up to nature, good and bad, and in nature or life few are the absolute hyprocrites. The men who decide the destinies of peoples are often not very intelligent, their convictions of right and wrong show a strange coincidence with their own profit, their own rule of kingly provinces. Like King Henry, they see right and justice in the fulfilling of their own wills. So Shakespeare could take from the old play, from the Chronicler, from the popular legend, his heroic conquering monarch, and heartily put him on the stage. Yet the poet's mirror did not reflect military glory only. Its image of the truth showed also the English soldier dead in the dunghill, the field grown up to weeds, and the infant spitted on the pike. In his imitation of life, the poet did not confine himself to one aspect or the other. So Henry V is not merely the happy warrior, nor is he merely a biting satire of the conqueror's ambition. In desire for an immediate and narrow unity, we are not to insist on one or the other only. We are to accept all three of the play's themes. First and most evident, the splendid conqueror of drum-and-trumpet patriotism is there to be hurrahed for. Yet by the comedy the bubbles of his glory now and then are pricked and he becomes no nobler than the thievish Pistol. Indeed those holding the conception of Henry the ideal Englishmen have tended to neglect the comedy; their play of a single heroic theme has no need for it. As parody of Henry's heroics, the comedy forms a bridge from the first of the play's themes to the second: the horrors resulting from the King's ambition. This second theme, as the history of criticism shows, has for some readers been so overshadowed by the first as to be concealed. The play, then, is not written merely to promote the views of Erasmus the pacifist. Though Henry is wet with innocent blood, he has, nevertheless, all the nobility possible to an immediately effective conqueror. His standards are not uncommon among men, and in their sincerity deserve sincere treatment. These two themes, then, by contrast enhance each other, to our pleasure as we view the whole. Then there is the third theme, that of king and people: the king worn with the care of his subjects, and the people under his charge carrying on the varied functions that fulfill Platonic justice.

The second theme and the third, Shakespeare's own addition to the historical story, are more obviously his own than what he adapted from Holinshed for the stage; we may even declare them his main interest. But even so, we need not hide from ourselves that in this work of art the various parts, independent or even contradictory, have in their self-subsistence such relation to each other that none of them can be spared.

DUKE UNIVERSITY

Elizabethan Belief in Spirits and Witchcraft

by ROBERT H. WEST

THE EDITOR of a widely-used teaching edition of Shakespeare's plays makes the statement in an appendix on witches and witchcraft that contrary to our popular supposition that every Englishman of Shakespeare's time believed in witches "actually there were far more sceptics than believers." "In general," he says, "most Englishmen scoffed at witchcraft, though with a sneaking suspicion that 'there might be something in it.' An Elizabethan play about witches thus produced much the same reaction in an audience as a modern horror film."[1]

The caution that not all the Elizabethan population believed in witches with a whole and simple faith is undoubtedly a good one; a modern writer on Shakespeare and the supernatural who calls the faith in witches 'universal' and says that it "forced a popular dramatist to adopt the current beliefs" has undoubtedly over-stated his case.[2] Especially among courtiers and other pretenders to the very latest style in beliefs, witchcraft no doubt lost ground in Jacobean times. If we may trust Francis Osborn, even King James gave up the superstition and would have eliminated its statutes from the books if he had thought the people were ready for the change.[3] Certainly in his reign his cherished Ben Johnson wrote and produced a highly rationalistic play which jeered freely at the whole notion of an effective confederacy between devils and human beings. Seventeen years earlier Samuel Harsnett had made very rough and sarcastic fun of the fraudulent practices of the dissenting devil-caster, John Darrell, and later of his Catholic prototype, the Jesuit Weston.[4]

But medieval writers, too, had been able to speak lightly about devils and witches, and the mere fact that the age of Shakespeare did not always speak seriously of them is no reliable sign that it was sufficiently emancipated from the belief in them to receive them in tragedies as nothing more than a melodramatic chill as we receive mad scientists in horror movies. The inescapable truth certainly is that the main body of surviving

---

1 *Shakespeare: 23 Plays and the Sonnets*, ed. G. B. Harrison (New York, 1948), pp. 1080-81.

2 Cumberland Clark, *Shakespeare and the Supernatural* (London, 1931), p. 33.

3 Francis Osborn, "Essay on Such as Condemn All they Understand not a Reason for," in *The Works of Francis Osborn* (London, 1673), p. 551.

4 Samuel Harsnett *A Discovery of the Fraudulent Practises of John Darrel* (London, 1599), and *A Declaration of Egregious Popish Impostures* (London, 1603).

Elizabethan comment on witchcraft and demonology is quite serious and, to our view, highly credulous. The genuine scepticism which occasionally appears is heavily offset either by evidence that it was not popular or by reservations plain in its context. It is hard to believe, for instance, that Harsnett was writing to any considerable body of contemporary opinion, for he lost ground in the controversy with Darrell and had to be relieved by two very earnest angelologists, who argued with the full apparatus of their 'science.'[5] Jonson's play, *The Devil is an Ass,* though it opens to derision a particular impeachment for witchcraft, is very far from seriously denying the devil or his malice and activity. Jonson's is virtually the only surviving devil play before 1642 that voices any genuine scepticism. Between *Dr. Faustus* and the *Late Lancashire Witches* we have, on the other hand, a dozen plays that, whatever their authors may really have believed, make very orthodox statements about witches and spirits. Non-dramatic literature by men like Spenser, Lodge, and Nashe does not afford a single notice of demonology that anyone could say was edged with thorough-going rationalism. Nashe does, of course, make some fun of demonology in *Pierce Penniless;* but he also translates there verbatim a long passage from a standard demonology. Lodge has his own pamphlet of demonology,[6] quite serious, and Spenser is too busy with the poetic values of demonological fancy to declare himself literally one way or another.

In the special Elizabethan literature of demonology some writers are more wary of devils than others and more savage against witches, but with the one stark exception of Reginald Scot, they all subscribe to the salient doctrines of demonology and witchcraft. When King James published his *Demonologie* in 1597 he may have had the seeds of a later private recantation in him, as Osborn claims, but he made, just the same, a firm assertion of all the essentials of the witch doctrine. The Essex minister, George Gifford, who is sometimes cried up as a rationalist, was tenderer than James toward the helpless rustics accused of *maleficium,* but he did not doubt the genuineness of the devil's power in the world.[7] Although Harsnett pokes such fun at the demonology of his opponents as caused the good Dr. Hutchinson to click his tongue deprecatingly as he gave witchcraft in England its *coup de grace* 120 years after Harsnett wrote,[8] yet Harsnett is speaking always not against demonology as such

---

5 John Deacon and John Walker, *Dialogicall Discourses of Spirits and Divels* (London, 1601), and *A Summarie Answere to all the Material Points in any of Master Darel his Bookes* (London, 1601).

6 Thomas Lodge, *The Divil Conjured* (London, 1596).

7 George Gifford, *A Discourse of the Subtle Practises of Devils by Witches and Sorcerers* (London, 1587), and *A Dialogue Concerning Witches* (London, 1593).

8 Francis Hutchinson, *An Historical Essay Concerning Witchcraft* (London, 1720). See the Dedication.

but as a learned demonologist against an ignorant one. William Perkins expressed doubt of some of the tests proposed for witches, but none whatever of the horrid fact of witchcraft as a pact with devils.[9]

However firm these men and others like them may have been, in public at least, for the main articles of the witch doctrine, they did all share one element that importantly paved the way for rationalism: with a single voice they disparaged the angelological elaborations of the Romanist middle ages and equally the extravagances of Platonistic demonographers of the Renaissance. The scholastic doctrines about the angelic orders and personal guardians and a limited worship owing to good angels, and the Platonists' claim that they knew angels by name in every corner of nature and could commune with them, received the reprobation of virtually every godly Protestant writer on spirits and witchcraft. The very care and exhaustiveness of the scholastic and Platonist inquiries was itself an affront to the reformers, a prying into matters which the eye has not seen, an intolerable puffing up of the wordly intellect. The fact itself of knowledge about angels seemed dangerous, as including a temptation to thrust them into a place alongside saints as mediators between God and man, as powers in themselves worth conciliating.

The impulse under which the reformers wrote had, of course, a long history. From patristic times through the prodigious medieval articulation, Christian angelology had gone more and more into the philosophic details of angels' substance and power and offices, always with the dominant purpose of showing their creaturely abilities and limitations in service or enmity to God and man. The ancient pagan tendency to make too much of spirits showed itself in various magical-minded sects, and some contrary tendency to doubt their existence or their power was perhaps always close to the surface to judge by the repeated complaints of all kinds of angelologists against Epicureans and Sadducees. The orthodox theologian was under pressure, then, at once to keep the doctrine of angels in check, lest it give rise to a false worship, and to elaborate it to prove its solidity and reasonableness. Between these two impulses the great scholastics had put together their rational scheme of angels, a scheme that by answering every question lucidly, cut the ground from under the magician, who profited by mystification in the doctrine of spirits, and from under the sceptic, who profited by confusion in it. Thomas Aquinas showed with perhaps more cogency than anyone before or after him how angels might be supposed to do much in nature without having complete sovereignty in it. He showed lucidly, too, that only evil angels would serve men's will-

9 William Perkins, "A Discourse of the Damned Art of Witchcraft," in *The Works* (London, 1609), vol. III.

ful appetites, and that any deliberate summoning of them amounted to sinful worship.

The Roman church allowed, however, a minor kind of worship to good angels as acknowledgement of their superior place in the scale of creatures, and this provision some Platonistic theorists of the Renaissance such as Cornelius Agrippa took as opening the door to theurgical practices like those described in the famous *Egyptian Mysteries* attributed to Iamblichus and translated into Latin by Ficino. The magic-minded Renaissance Platonists magnified extremely the part angels had in the world and the means of man's access to them. Without quite returning to the entire Neo-Platonic theory of demons, they very much disordered the accurate scholastic rationale, particularly by a shadowy but insistent contention that a man could come inevitably to God through angels by a sort of resistless, graduated identification of himself with each member in turn of the rising chain of the angelic orders. This theurgical road to salvation by-passed orthodox theological emphasis on obedience to God's will and showed the angel in something of the Neo-Platonic style as a being wholly determined by his place in the chain of being and responsive almost of necessity to suitable stimulus.

Protestant theologians, then, professing to see twin dangers in Catholic and Platonistic theorizing, set out to sweep away all angel-worshippers at once by damning the presumption and inquisitiveness of all. Protestants minimized angels largely by boasting ignorance of the details which Scholastics and Platonists had labored with. We must not claim, says one Protestant theologian after another, to understand clearly angels' nature or the means of their action, for these things are obscure in Scripture. Lambert Daneau, one of Calvin's contemporaries and supporters, complains bitterly against the influential Jesuit angelogist, Maldonat, "a man, as you perceaue, of euyll name," who has disputed "curiously of these matters, proposing this theame openly, and publishing a Book, wherein he professeth that he will intreate of Deuilles." Daneau rejects "these vayne babling proofes, and curious disputations . . ." He abhors devils and will not try to say what they are like or how organized or of what colors, or any other such trifles, which "by them is more exquisitely and diligently handled, which would be acompted of the more subtil sort among the scholastical doctores . . ." "I enuie not at it," says Daneau, "and I easily yield them the knowledge of such oglie matters."[10]

Calvin himself, though admitting in the *Institute* that we must rehearse the lore of angels so far as Scripture gives the means, puts as his chief reason for it that "it is very necessary for the confuting of many errors";

10 Lambert Daneau, *A Dialogue of Witches* (London, 1575), Introduction, B4.

". . . we must leaue those vanities that idel men haue taught without
warrant of the worde of God, concerning the nature, degrees, and multitude of angels."[11] In his commentaries Calvin rarely passes an opportunity
to disparage the medieval readings on angels. Above all, he says, we must
not credit angels with the deeds that are God's, as Platonists and Romanists
do: "Those men do deale wickedly and peruersely who feign that the
Angels haue something of their own, or who make them Mediatours betweene God and us, in such sort that they doe darken the power of God,
being as it were set far off . . . Therefore we must beware of those doting
speculations of Plato, because God is too farre distant from us, we must
goe unto the Angels . . ."[12] "The whole glory must be ascribed to God
alone, we are to acknowledge the Angels but his instruments, for otherwise
wee should easilie slip into the error of the Papists, who ascribing more
than is meete to them, doe rob God of his power to clothe them with
it . . ."[13]

Undoubtedly these reforming sneers at Scholastics and Platonics as
mere weavers of moonbeams helped to prepare the way for rationalism,
and a good sign of it is the close adherence to the Protestant theologians
in tone and in much doctrine of the sceptical Kentish squire, Reginald
Scot. In Shakespeare's England—and in fact, in England for nearly a
hundred years after Shakespeare was dead—Scot was about the most
uncompromising rationalist to publish on spirits and witchcraft. Just how
uncompromising he was is hardly appreciated to this day among Shakespeare scholars. Most who mention him are still inclined to say with the
late Professor Schelling that he "did not venture to deny the existence
of witchcraft . . ."[14] This opinion rests on a much-quoted sentence from
Scot: "My question is not (as manie fondlie suppose) whether there be
witches or naie: but whether they can doo such miraculous works as are
imputed to them."[15] By this Scot meant that it would be idle to deny the
indisputable fact that many persons admitted to being witches and in a
sense might properly be called witches, but that the true question was
whether the witch had the wordly service of devils as was claimed for her.
"I can call spirits from the vasty deep," says Glendower. "Why so can I,
or so can any man. But will they come when you do call for them?" That
is Scot's question and he asks it as sceptically as Hotspur did. He consistently denies all the outstanding doctrines about demonic activity in the

---

11 John Calvin, *The Institutes* (London, 1580), I, xiv, 44.
12 *The Holy Gospel of Jesus Christ, according to John with the Commentary of M. John
Calvin,* trans. Christopher Teetherstone (London, 1584), on chapter v, verse 4.
13 *A Commentarie upon the Prophecie of Isaiah by Mr. John Calvin,* trans. by C. C.
(London, 1609), on chapter xxxvii, verse 36.
14 F. E. Schelling, *Shakespeare and Demi-Science* (Philadelphia, 1927), p. 159.
15 Reginald Scot, *The Discoverie of Witchcraft,* ed. Brinsley Nicholson (London, 1886),
The Epistle, p. xvii.

physical world, and so goes far beyond his successor, John Webster, and even beyond Thomas Hobbes.

To help out his argument — and perhaps to protect himself — Scot deliberately adopts the Calvinist tone against Catholic and Platonist experts in devil-lore. All the Calvinist arguments, too, he uses, with generous and respectful identification of himself with their great originators. Entirely in the Calvinist convention he makes great play on the difficulty of knowing anything about beings so remote as angels. He pours the usual scorn on all the scholastical doctors who talk as though they had visited heaven. He ranges himself virtuously with St. Paul and St. Augustine and other great men who had expressed reservations, and he rests with them upon Scripture and confines himself with them to consideration of those things needful to salvation. He repeatedly cites Calvin to justify his general attitude, and quotes him and Peter Martyr and other Protestant authors to support his ridicule of scholastic and Platonic elaborations. He speaks strongly in the usual Protestant tone against worship of angels, the doctrine of guardians, and the Dionysian orders. Worship he links scornfully to paganism.[16] For guardians, he says, "there is not reason in nature, nor authorities in scripture," and he quotes Calvin on how shameful it is to refer to a single angel the care God has for every one of us.[17] As for Dionysius, either, says Scot, he "Followed his owne imaginations and conceipts, or else the corruptions of that age"; Calvin makes it plain how little we should trust Dionysius.[18] The "schoole doctors" pretend that some orders of angels are not sent into the world and that archangels are sent only about great matters whereas "angels are common hacknies about evere trifle . . ."[19] These are "fond imaginations" and "impious curiosities."

Scot takes care to make plain that he himself believes in angels; he can be indignant against the Sadducees, "impious and fond," who say that "divels are onelie motions and affections, and that angels are but tokens of God's power." For his part, he will "confesse with *Augustine*" that these matters are above his "reach and capacitie: and yet so farre as God's word teacheth" he "will not stick to saie, that they are living creatures, ordeined to serve the Lord in their vocation. And although they abode not in their first estate, yet that they are the Lord's ministers, and executioners of his wrath, to trie and tempt in this world, and to punish the reprobate in hell fier in the world to come."[20]

Scot holds that the assault of the devils is "spiritual,"[21] and in this too he sounds (as he takes care by repeated citation of great Protestants to make

---

16 *A Discourse of Divels and Spirits,* ed. Brinsley Nicholson (London, 1886), ii, 413.
17 Ibid., x, 424.
18 Ibid., vii, 420.
19 Ibid., x, 424.
20 Ibid., xxxi, 453; also x, 424.
21 Ibid., xii, 426.

himself sound) as though he were in received Protestant tradition. But
it is just here that Scot leaves that tradition, for when he says that angelic
activities are spiritual he means to deny totally that they are ever in any
sense bodily. This is a stand which Scot never compromises, and with it he
totally rejects witchcraft, magic, apparition, celestial management, and
virtually everything else that comes under the heading of 'operation' in
the demonologies. He is silent about the angel's ability to handle the
humors and so control a man's fancy internally. When most Protestant
angelologists speak of a "spiritual" contact between man and angel, they
may mean this secret suggesting through the humors. What Scot means
he never says in physiological terms; but he does not ever concede to
angels any kind of physical rule of anything. He notes that Paul "biddeth
us put on the whole armour of God," and like many great theologians
interprets it allegorically. But he does not, like most of them, allow that
this allegorical armor has ever to turn a bodily assault. Whatever biblical
references demonologists use to show angels physically active, says Scot,
are either grossly misquoted (as when Jean Bodin claims that an angel
slew the first-born of Egypt, whereas the text says God did it)[22] or are
misinterpreted (as when the name *Lucifer* in Isaiah 14 is thought to
signify Satan instead of Nebuchadnezzar, as the plain sense is). Genuine
biblical references to spirits are best taken as figures of speech, Scot says,
else we might suppose that the devil really goes about roaring like a lion,
although what the Bible says of his lion-likeness "is ment of the soule
and spirituall devouring, as verie novices in religion may judge."[24] If "we
have onelie respect to the bare word, or rather to the letter, where spirits
or divels are spoken of in the scriptures, we shall run into . . . dangerous
absurdities . . . For some are so carnallie minded that a spirit is no sooner
spoken of, but immediatelie they thinke of a blacke man with cloven feet,
a pair of hornes, a taile, clawes, and eies as broad as a bason." Surely
the devil would not be so foolish, even if he had the power, as to show
himself in an ugly form.[25]

But, thinks Scot, he does not have the power to show any form. "His
essence also and his forme is so proper and peculiar (in mine opinion) unto
himself, as he himself cannot alter it, but must needs be content therewith,
as with that which God hath ordeined for him, and assigned unto him, as
peculiarlie as he hath given to us our substance without power to alter
the same at our pleasures. For we find not that a spirit can make a bodie,
more than a bodie can make a spirit: The spirit of God excepted, which

22 Ibid., xviii 434.
23 Ibid., viii, 421.
24 Ibid., xxxii, 455; xxxi, 453; xiii, 427.
25 Ibid., xi, 426.

is omnipotent."[26] As for the testimony of those who claim to have seen apparitions or works of witchcraft, "See whether the witnesses be not single of what credit, sex, and age they are; namelie lewd, miserable, and envious poore people; most of them which speake to anie purpose being old women, & children of the age of 4. 5. 6. 7. 8. or 9. yeares."[27]

Scot notices rather vaguely the distinction between the scholastic view that by an ordinary power angels "can assume & take unto them bodies at their pleasure: of which mind all papists and some protestants are . . .," and the opinion of "another sort," less gross, "which hold, that such bodies are made to their hands . . . "[28] He was here on dangerous ground, since virtually every great Protestant commentator was one of these sorts. In a chapter of hardly half a page Scot merely sneers at the diversity of demonological opinion and quotes Peter Martyr very disingenuously to leave the false impression that as Peter criticized some theories of apparition he denied apparition itself.

Scot himself did deny flatly all demonic apparition and equally the kindred phenomenon of demonic possession, even that of the serpent by Satan in Paradise. "Indeed we saie, and saie trulie, to the wicked, The divell is in him: but we meane not thereby, that a reall divell is gotten into his guts . . ." Scot read Genesis to mean not that Satan entered the serpent, but that when the Bible said *serpent* it signified Satan. The Bible, he explains, asserts only that the serpent seduced Eve, and that against him the curse went out. If it meant that Satan controlled the serpent, who was afterwards punished for it, then it chronicled a great injustice to the snake in very misleading language. Obviously Genesis speaks metaphorically: ". . . the divell is resembled to an odious creature, who as he creepeth upon us to annoie our bodies; so doth the divell there creepe into the conscience of *Eve,* to abuse and deceive her . . ." Though in consideration of our feeble capacities this event is described as a "materiall tragedie," we are not to think it really was so.[29]

Plainly Scot was nothing of a scientific rationalist such as rose in the next century; but plainly too he brought to even biblical evidence of angels an independent judgment that enabled him to confront the angelological tradition more unflinchingly than could even such a scientist as Robert Boyle. Scot was not, like Boyle, merely sidling away from angelology because it was unserviceable to a particular kind of wordly inquiry. He was hacking at the very bole of what, like other Protestants, he thought

26 Ibid., xxxii, 454.
27 Ibid., xxxiii, 455.
28 Ibid., xvii, 433.
29 Ibid., xxxi, 452.

an absurdly proliferated growth which, unlike most others, he believed would best be cut back to the very root.

No doubt Scot represented a strong body of contemporary opinion. But at the same time the thing most striking of all about him is his uniqueness. Not another man of his time in England or on the continent that I know of published anything like so unflinchingly direct a blow at the demonology that was the indispensable condition of the witch doctrine. If that doctrine was truly a laughing stock to the educated of Shakespeare's time, or nothing more than a kind of thriller fiction, surely it could not have continued to claim victims and to have the support of the learned clear through the seventeenth century. More writers would have come out against it than the handful we can count, and that handful would have been less deprecatory than most of them were, more positive, more wedded, as Scot was, to an inflexible rejection of the work of angels in the physical world, whether good or evil.

Yet the Protestant distaste for speculative demonology did give a margin to scepticism, a margin within which very assertive and derisory doubts of some doctrines and some authorities of demonology could be freely expressed. Such doubts may well have colored the whole attitude of Elizabethan play-goers and playwrights toward witchcraft, though without sapping appreciably the genuine, literal abhorrence for witch and demon.

UNIVERSITY OF GEORGIA

Lyrical Instrumentation in Marlowe:
A Step Towards Shakespeare

by ANTS ORAS

I

Oᴺᴇ of the most significant changes in our attitude towards the literary art of the Elizabethans is probably a growing awareness of the conscious, disciplined way in which these knowledgeable students of the rules of rhetoric handled style and expression. We recognize their intimate familiarity with a bewildering multitude of well-defined figures of speech as well as the ease with which they found their way about a complicated system of traditional symbolic imagery. The notion of untutored genius has receded into the background in our approach to their literary methods. At least one field remains, however, in which this change of attitude is still rather incomplete. The admirable quality of the verbal music in a great deal of Elizabethan verse is fully acknowledged, but it is here that too much is perhaps still somewhat one-sidedly attributed to the unaccountable accident of genius alone and too little to the science of which genius knows so well how to avail itself. The rhythms and rhymes of the Elizabethans have been explored, though by no means fully. Their more conspicuous uses of consonantal patterns, such as alliteration, have attracted some expert attention. However, all but a few scholars and a poet or two have stopped short of a closer look at their treatment of that other, far more elusive element of language, the vowels[1]. This may be partly because of considerable changes of pronunciation that have made it difficult or impossible to recognize some of their vowel patterns unless one becomes at least a passable linguist. Some thirty or forty years ago even linguistics would often have been very misleading as a help in such inquiries. But the situation has changed. Henry Cecil Wyld, Otto Jespersen, Daniel Jones, Wilhelm Franz, Helge Kökeritz—to name only a few—have blazed many trails through the wilderness. A more intent examination of Elizabethan vowel arrangements now seems to suggest that these were frequently produced with a care not unlike that with which a painter applies his paints or a musician his sequences of sound. Not only in their rhymed poetry but also in their blank verse, beautiful and often amazingly geo-

---

1 See, e.g., Ulrich I. Goldsmith, "Words out of a Hat? Alliteration and Assonance in Shakespeare's Sonnets." *JEGP,* XLIX (1950), 33-48; Edith Sitwell, *A Notebook on William Shakespeare* (London, 1948); and some good remarks in A. Stein, "Structures of Sound in Donne's Verse," *Kenyon Review,* XIII (1951), 20 ff. and 256 ff.

metrical vowel designs give every indication of attentive, deliberate craftsmanship.

The beginnings of such an approach in blank verse coincide precisely with the first emergence of this verse form in English. From the very first line of Surrey's translations of Virgil to the last, a technique of vowel echoes is employed which makes up for many deficiencies in his handling of rhythm.[2] The effects he achieved by his chiming repetitions of the same sounds, usually in prominent metrical positions, can be very vivid. He frequently links long successions of lines by assonance, near-rhyme and rhyme, generally placing these echoes before well-marked metrical pauses, and massing them or thinning them out as the rhetorical and emotional temperature rises or declines. Much of the poetical appeal of his verse is due to this musical approach, for which he may have received stimuli from the Italians or, up to a point, from Virgil himself. His immediate successors imitated him in this procedure, but as a rule not too successfully because of their relative lack of phonetic (and poetic) imagination. Their heavy, monotonously distributed pauses, usually placed after the fourth, often the sixth, and almost invariably the tenth, final, syllable of the line, became even heavier under the weight of ponderously reiterated sound. The first six lines of *Gorboduc* may serve as a fair, and not altogether unattractive, example of this method:[3]

    Vid. The silent night, that brings the quiet *pawse*
    From painefull trauailes of the wearie *day,*
    Prolonges my carefull *thoughtes,* and makes me *blame*
    The slowe Au*rore,* that so for loue or *shame*
    Doth long de*lay* to *shewe* her blushing *face;*
    And now the *day* re*newes* my griefull *plaint.*

The distinctly marked, slow tune in these verses owes much to a pronounced pattern of vowel echoes, partly passing into rhyme, which emphasizes the stress before all but two of the principal pauses both in the middle and at the end of the lines. The result is careful rhythmical balance, interrupted movement, and lack of momentum—declamatory dignity indeed, but also slow monotony. This may suit the mood of this speech, but there are so many similar, and often long, passages in *Gorboduc* that the total effect is dragging and uninspired. This impression agrees with the lack of flexibility, the wearying uniformity of pattern characterizing the rhythm, the syntax and the rhetoric of this and most other early blank verse.

---

2 See A. Oras, "Surrey's Technique of Phonetic Echoes: A Method and its Background," *JEGP*, L (1951), 289-308.
3 Quoted according to J. W. Cunliffe, *Early English Classical Tragedies* (Oxford, 1912).

II

It took a finer ear and a more resilient and inventive mind—in fact, a verse musician of genius—to instil new life into this unexciting technique. Such men as George Gascoigne, Thomas Hughes, Thomas Kyd, or even George Peele and Robert Greene, hardly met these specifications. A man of far superior talent, Christopher Marlowe, had to come to make phonetic instrumentation serve higher imaginative purposes. It is of course in his *Tamburlaine* that he first emerges as a highly effective, inspired poet. There we have him full-fledged—exuberantly rhetorical or lyrical; sometimes verging on the grotesque in his search for extreme effects but nearly always powerful; not too varied but original and impressive; and impressive to a large extent because of the stirring sound of his verse.

What had happened to that sound? One things seems certain: Marlowe had become much more fully alive than his predecessors to the advantages of dynamically handled phonetic organization. He saw that echoes could be so arranged as to accelerate the forward movement of the verse rather than slow it up. Like the authors of *Gorboduc,* he often marks the usual caesural positions by emphatic echoes, but the result is different. Listen for instance to Tamburlaine magniloquently asserting his greatness to Zenocrate, who has just been insulted by Bajazeth's wife, Zabina. It should be difficult not to notice the repetition, at measured intervals, of the same vowels, and partly the same consonants, nearly always in the fourth, sixth or tenth syllable as in *Gorboduc,* but producing the impression of a steady onward surge:

> And calme the rage of thundring Iupi*ter*:
> Sit downe by *her*: adorned with my Crowne,
> As if thou *wert* the Empresse of the *world*.
> Stir not Zenocra*te* vntill thou *see*
> Me martch victorious*ly* with all my men,
> Triumphing ouer *him* and these his *kings,*
> Which I will *bring* as Vassals to thy feete.
> Til then take thou my crowne, vaunt of my *worth*,
> And manage *words* with *her* as we will armes.

(1221-9)

Seven expressions, all in stressed positions, and mostly alliterating, dominate this passage with their distinctive *r*-colored vowels[4] (*Iupiter, her, wert,*

---

4 This quotation, like all others from Marlowe, is according to C. F. Tucker Brooke's Oxford edition of 1910. Phonology does not appear to have reached any agreement as to the extent to which the specific quality of vowels followed by an *r* had become obscured in the sixteenth century. The rhymes suggest, however, that at least as early as in Surrey, vowels whose quality originally differed could be considered sufficiently similar to be used for rhyming purposes if they occurred before a preconsonantal or final *r*. See "Surrey's Technique," note 2, and compare Marlowe's own rhymes, e.g., *first, worst* (*Ovid's El.,* II.6.39-40); *worth, birth* (ibid., II.16.37,38); *sterne, turne* (an internal rhyme,

world, worth, words, her), but the ear is not wearied since other sequences intervene. An effect of energetic progression is created by making the echoes follow each other in unbroken wave-like series of three or four, extending through two or three lines which are thus welded into one uninterrupted rhythmical movement. These waves of approximately equal length and largely parallel structure succeed one another sufficiently often to produce the illusion of a long, sweeping advance, like that of an army on the march—a notion which the speech itself explicitly suggests. As soon as this result is achieved, Marlowe abandons this pattern and changes his methods.

Here, as on various other occasions, Marlowe's echoes are predominantly within the verse line. One of his most important innovations, however, is his greatly extended use of *final* phonetic correspondences. Concentrating his principal phonetic effects into his line endings, he increases the compactness cf the line as a rhythmical unit unimpeded in its flow by much internal segmentation. Most of his internal echoes tend to reinforce his terminal effects. Moreover, by carrying his echoes from one verse ending to another, he is capable of linking passages of considerable length into coherent lyrical or rhetorical structures of remarkable musical force, often leading up to a striking phonetic climax. The existence in Marlowe's work of such lyrical organisms, so complete in themselves as almost to be detachable from their dramatic context, has repeatedly been recognized, but their phonetic organization has hardly ever been examined.[5]

In an article published in the *Philological Quarterly* for January, 1945,[6] Paul H. Kocher propounded and defended the argument that the famous soliloquy on Zenocrate and beauty in 1 *Tamb.* 1916-70, "contains embedded in its structure what appears to be a blank verse adaptation of one of Marlowe's own sonnets." His main reasons are that this passage consists of fourteen lines; that it seems complete in itself; that it falls into sections roughly corresponding to those of an Elizabethan sonnet; and that it has a final rhymed couplet. He also recalls certain borrowings from Spenser in *Tamburlaine* in which the final rhymes of the Spenserian stanza are retained, and concludes that in this lyric eulogy on beauty, Marlowe may, though with similar incompleteness, have reduced to blank verse another rhymed composition, this time not by Spenser but by himself. One should, however, look more closely at the passage in question. It will

ibid., 1.6.57). Shakespeare has, e.g.: *stir, spur* (*Ven. & Ad.*, 283,285); *birds, herds* (ibid., 455,456); *curst, first* (ibid., 887,888); *worshipper, fear* (*Rape of Lucr.*, 86,88). What applies to rhyme should likewise hold good of the less rigidly established technique of more approximate echoes.

5 See C. F. Tucker Brooke, "Marlowe's Versification and Style," *SP*, XIX (1922), 186-205, as well as the article referred to in note 6.

6 "A Marlowe Sonnet," 39-45.

appear that while it perhaps is even more like a sonnet than Professor
Kocher suggests, it shows a perfectly consistent technique of a kind not
mentioned by him, illustrating and supplementing much of what has been
said here:

> What is beauty saith my sufferings *then?*
> If all the pens that euer poets *held,*
> Had fed the feeling of their maisters thoughts,
> And euery sweetnes that inspir'd their harts,
> Their minds, and muses on admyred *theames:*
> If all the heauenly Quintessence they *still*
> From their immortall flowers of Poe*sy,*
> Wherein as in a myrrour we per*ceiue*
> The highest reaches of a humaine *wit.*
> If these had made one Poems period
> And all combin'd in Beauties worthi*nesse,*
> Yet should ther houer in their restlesse *heads,*
> One thought, one grace, one woonder at the *least,*
> Which into words no vertue can di*gest* . . .

(1941-54)

Looking at the vowels in the line endings of this passage, we find that
its final echoes are by no means restricted to the rhyme in the last couplet.
All but three of these endings are linked by assonance. Eight of the four-
teen have the vowels $[\epsilon] \sim [\bar{e}]$,[7] and three, the vowel $[\text{I}]$. If the quantitative differences in vowels of identical or similar quality are disregarded,
as was often done by Marlowe and his contemporaries in their rhymes,[8]
we get three assonantal groups which accord precisely with the main syntactic subdivisions: one of five lines with three endings in $[\epsilon] \sim [\bar{e}]$, one
of four lines with three endings in $[\text{I}]$ and one ending in $[\bar{e}]$, and a final
one of five lines with four endings in $[\epsilon] \sim [\bar{e}] = 5 + 4 + 5$. In other
words, we have a balanced structure of three stanza-like sections, the
endings of each of which are dominated by one vowel. If the three echoless
endings are marked as *x,* the total pattern is *aaxxa, bbab, xaaaa.* Furthermore, there is phonetic gradation in this arrangement, since consonance,
at first only partial (worthi*nesse,* hea*ds*), then complete (lea*st,* dige*st*),
does not appear in the echoes until close to the end: the most strongly
marked echoes are reserved for the final effect. The transition from asson-

---

7 The vowel in *theames, perceiue* and *least* was a long ϵ-type sound; the vowel in *harts*
was also a front vowel and may have been associated, if not identified, in Marlowe's
phonetic consciousness with the (ϵ) or $(\ddot{e})$ group, in which case the terminal pattern
would be even more balanced: *aaxaa, bbab, xaaaa.*

8 See Marlowe's own practice in rhyming, e.g. *throne, vpon (Hero & Leander,* I.7,8); *feast,
guest* (ibid., I.93 94); *reapt, kept* (ibid., I.327,328); *yeeld, held* (ibid., II.83,84); *giue,
grieue (Ovid's El.,* I.3.17,18).

ance to rhyme, then, is gradual. Hence much of the impression of inevita-
bility which the conclusion creates: it is amply prepared for by the handling
of sound in the earlier endings. The final rhymed couplet consequently
does not come as a surprise. The crescendo movement is quite distinct;
the phonetic and the poetical culmination coincide.

These fourteen lines constitute, in effect, an assonantal sonnet, somewhat different, but not very different, from the orthodox pattern, more
lyrical perhaps than most of the rhymed sonnets of the period, but firmly
designed, and concluding with a flourish, emotional as well as phonetic,
as Elizabethan sonnets used to do. Nevertheless, it may still be doubted
whether this resemblance was intentional. It may merely have been one
of the flukes not uncommon with writers of genius. If it was, this fluke
was repeated in the second part of the play, in an even more compact
and better developed form. The passage just examined is about beauty—
the most impassioned utterance on the subject in Part One. The beginning
of Tamburlaine's soliloquy in 2 *Tamb*. II.iii resumes the theme of Zenocrate's beauty, this time associating it with the notion of death. The first
fourteen lines (the figure seems significant)—again well-rounded like
a separate lyric—read as follows:

> Blacke is the beauty of the brightest *day,*
> The golden balle of heauens eternal *fire,*
> That danc'd with glorie on the siluer *waues*:
> Now wants the fewell that enflamde his *beames*
> And all with faintnesse and for foule dis*grace,*
> He bindes his temples with a frowning *cloude,*
> Ready to darken earth with endlesse *night*:
> Zenocrate that gaue him light and *life,*
> Whose eies shot fire from their Iuory *bowers,*
> And tempered euery soule with liuely *heat,*
> Now by the malice of the angry *Skies,*
> Whose iealousie admits no second *Mate,*
> Drawes in the comfort of her latest *breath*
> All dasled with the hellish mists of *death.*
>   (2969-82)

Three vowel motifs, [ē] ∼ [ɛ̄],[9] [ɔɪ] (or [eɪ]) and [ɔʊ] (or [oʊ]),[10] are
here arranged in an unbroken echo pattern: *abaaa, cbbc, abaaa* — again
5 + 4 + 5. As in the previous passage, the four middle lines, placed in
the exact center, have an arrangement of their own, partly contrasted

---

9 The vowel in *beames, heat* is much as in *waues, Mate,* etc.; length in *breath, death* seems
the preferred poetical form at least until Drayton. See H. C. Wyld, *Studies in English
Rhymes* (London, 1923), pp. 89ff.
10 The equivalent of present-day [ai] apparently had no *a*-quality in its first component.
Its exact quality, like that of the counterpart of our [au], is impossible to determine.

with the rest, with which, however, they are neatly linked by the [ɔɪ] (or [eɪ]) echoes. The five lines preceding this arrangement and the five lines following it are identical in their terminal design. The total structure approaches symmetry even more closely than the one discussed before: it can be divided into two balanced halves of equal length coinciding with the principal syntactic divisions. As before, the last five lines show distinct intensification of phonetic similarity: the crescendo method of phonetic gradation is maintained. This time the final section has two rhymes: *heat, Mate* and *breath, death,* but the effect of the last rhyme is especially strong because of the closer grouping. This design is even shapelier than the previous one, but the main outlines have undergone but little change. The entire passage looks remarkably like a second, more deliberate attempt to produce the same kind of lyrical structure, but with even more symmetry, as well as with a particularly distinct application of a crescendo technique.[11]

The resemblance of these two passages to sonnets can hardly be denied. Whether Marlowe himself thought of them as sonnets is another question. The important point is, in any case, that his sense of design should have been displayed in two structures of such striking similarity, combining careful equipoise with such consistency of climactic gradation. The fact that the second attempt so scrupulously adds the finishing touches to the outline adumbrated in the earlier "sonnet" reveals Marlowe in the unexpected rôle of a formal perfectionist. This meticulous regard for form becomes even clearer when we examine his internal assonances, which mostly reinforce the final ones, sometimes closely preceding them: *"frown*ing *cloude," "enflamde* his *beames," "gaue* him *light* and *life,/* Whose *eies* shot *fire* from their *Iuory* bowers." The result is a vividness of orchestration not encountered in any earlier blank verse. The lyricism of the poetry is greatly intensified by the powerfully patterned sound.

Symmetry and balance, however, even though working up toward a climactic effect, hardly represent the essential Marlowe. Intensity, impulsively kindling into even greater intensity, seemingly on an ever ascending scale, appears far more typical of his art, at least in *Tamburlaine*. As we continue the reading of the second soliloquy, we find that the "sonnet," however effective, is merely a beginning, and that the echo technique is to be adapted to even greater heights of lyrical fervor. The rest of the speech, or rather lyrical chant, centers round the name of Zenocrate, and

---

11 The conclusions suggested by this analysis differ from those drawn by Tucker Brooke when he says that Marlowe's assonance "almost suggests that the poet has difficulty in preventing himself from falling into regular rime" ("Marlowe's Versification," 195). Like his predecessors, Marlowe appears to have known very well what degree of phonetic similarity he chose to employ. His echoes are not awkward survivals of a rhyming tradition but elements in a more extensive, complex organization of sound.

the farther we get, the more often that name is echoed both inside the lines and in the line endings. Assonance is intensified into rhyme, and the conclusion is again formed by a rhymed couplet, with the chief theme of the passage as the crowning finale:

The Cheru*bins* and holy Sera*phins*
That *sing* and play before the *king* of *kings,*
Vse all their voices and their instruments
To entertaine diuine Zenocra*te.*
And in this *sweet* and currious harmo*ny,*
The God that tunes this musicke to our soules:
Holds out his hand in highest maies*ty*
To entertaine diuine Zenocra*te.*
Then let some holy trance conuay my thoughts,
Vp to the pallace of th' imperiall heauen:
That this my life may *be* as short to *me*
As are the daies of *sweet* Zenocra*te* . . .
(2994-3005)

III

What has so far been considered in Marlowe are "purple patches," passages apparently wrought with unusual care to produce particularly dazzling effects and accordingly not wholly representative of his average technique. But while the method in the bulk of his verse is somewhat less concentrated and intensive and his virtuosity less conspicuous, the tendencies are the same almost throughout. Literally from the first line of the first scene of Part One to the last line of Part Two, clusters of terminal correspondences, often dense, and not infrequently solidified into rhyme or near-rhyme, help to prolong the roll of the line endings,[12] internal echoes often support them, and certain dominant words, or groups of words, are every now and again accompanied by echoing expressions. Marlowe's lyrical use of refrain-like devices has been noticed, but no mention appears to have been made of the fact that the final vowels of such refrains or semi-refrains often dominate the phonetic design of the passages in which they occur. Tucker Brooke calls attention to Zenocrate's lament over Bajazeth and Zabina as an example of the way in which in Marlowe "the perfect single line . . . forms the theme of a burst of sustained emotion, which plays about it and often repeats it as a refrain."[13] This play of emotion about the repeated line—in this instance: "Behold the Turke and his great Emperesse"—is shown in the reverberations of the final

---

12 The first seven endings of 1 *Tamb.* I.i are: *agreeu'd, same, speech, Lords, I, age, Conquerors = abacxbc.* The last eleven endings of 2 *Tamb.* are: *selfe, Phaeton, farewel, see, company, die, end, fruit, fire, deplore, more = axabbcaxcdd.*
13 See "Marlowe's Versification," 190.

vowel of the refrain through the other line endings of the passage:

In feare and feeling of the like dis*tresse,*
Behold the Turke and his great Empe*resse.*
Ah myghty Ioue and holy Maho*met,*
Pardon my loue, oh pardon his con*tempt,*
Of earthly fortune, and respect of pitie,
And let not conquest ruthlessly pursewde
Be equally against his life in*censt,*
In this great Turke and haplesse Empe*resse.*

(2143-50)

In the equally well-known scene with the burden: "And ride in triumph through Persepolis" (1*Tamb*. II.v), the key-word carrying along with it a train of final echoes is *Persepolis: purposes* (742), *Persepolis* (745), *vsurie* (748), *wish* (753), *Persepolis* (754), *Persepolis* (755), *King* (758), *Persepolis* (759), *King* (762). In another flamboyant scene, showing Callapine with the rulers of the Near East flocking to offer him their troops for the destruction of Tamburlaine, the vowels of the last words of two refrain-like formulae, *majesty* and *men,* are used altogether twenty times in a passage of twenty-eight lines (3532-59).[14] In the coronation scene of Amyras, close before the end of the play (4583-4612), an effect approaching that of a refrain is achieved by making the verses conclude, at intervals (repeatedly at speech endings)[15], with polysyllables of a dactylic rhythm in [ɪ] or [i] : *dignity, souerainty, magnanimitie, necessity, maiesty, necessity, agony, Zenocrate, recouery, cruelty*—ten instances within thirty lines. Except for the name of Zenocrate, these words are all abstract nouns charged with emotional connotations. Similarity of sound and rhythm is coupled with resemblance in meaning, grammatical function and emotional tone. The relevance of this method in organizing the rhythm of the scene and adding to its lyrical resonance is difficult to miss.

In all these cases, as in many others, long passages are held together by an organization which is essentially musical, and often lyrical. The parallelism of sound, often of rhythm, and not infrequently (as in the last example) of grammatical category, meaning, and tone, contributes to the total impression of a chant, almost of recitative. The essential

---

14 The endings are: *men, esteem'd, Ierusalem, men, maiesty, bounds, Metropolis, Semyramis, horse, Maiesty, lesse, Bythinians, more, meane, victory, maiesty, repair'd, land, foot, maiestie, esteem'd, men, death, field, sacrifice, Mahomet, firmament, enemies.* Disregarding the quantitative differences, we get the pattern *abaabxbbxbaxxabbxxxbbaabxaab.*

15 For a pattern of similar speech endings see: *chiualry* (3755), *magnanimity* (3759), *maiesty* (3764), *Maiesty* (3771). Rhythmical subdivision, often almost in the manner of stanzas, is achieved also within speeches by the use of assonant words of parallel rhythmical structure, e.g., *Distinie* (2015), *extasies* (2019), *slaueries* (2022); *supremacie* (3127), *dignities* (3129), *infamies* (3130), *inconstancie* (3140); *Siria* (200), *Egyptia* (202), *Medea* (208), *Affrica* (212); *Asia* (936), *Persea* (939), *Asia* (941), *Grecia* (942), *Affrica* (946,), *Grecia* (947), etc.

elements of a passage are emphasized by phonetic means, as they in rhymed verse are brought into more vivid relief by the the rhymes. Close parallels could be found in the technique of modern opera.

Another significant application of this method of the phonetic leading motif appears in connection with the names of Zenocrate and Tamburlaine. Of the forty-two instances in which the former occurs in line endings, at least twenty-three belong within distinct patterns of terminal echoes, often composed of words with a similar dactylic (or pyrrhic) conclusion.[16] One such pattern has just been referred to. Other sequences are, e.g.: *misery, Zenocrate* (2152, 2153); *thee, me, Zenocrate* (2197, 2198, 2200); *Zenocrate, thee, free* (2215, 2217, 2218); *Zenocrate, victory* (2225, 2227); *Emperies, Zenocrate, see, inchastity* (2263, 2266, 2267, 2268); *deed, Zenocrate* (2285, 2288); *victories, Zenocrate* (2295, 2298) —all from the last scene of Part One. Less often, but not seldom, internal correspondences echo Zenocrate's name: "Disdaines Zenocra*te* to liue with *me*?" (78); "Stir not Zenocra*te* vntill thou *see*/ Me martch victorious*ly*" (1224-5); "To let them *see* (diuine Zenocra*te*)" 1666); "Wretched Zenocra*te*, that liuest to *see*" (2101); "Ah what may chance to *thee* Zenocra*te*?" (2153). This musical name, with an ending to which correspondences abound in the language, lends itself readily to such treatment. But exactly the same approach is noticeable in regard to the name of the conqueror himself. In the light of the previous observations, it should be difficult to put down to mere accident the fact that in more than one-third of the passages in which his name occurs, the long [ē] of its final syllable is repeated in closely juxtaposed words placed in emphatic metrical positions. Quite often the consonants are likewise echoed. This occurs in the very first lines of the prologue to Part One:

> From iygging *vaines* of riming mother wits,
> And such con*ceits* as clownage keepes in *pay,*
> Weele *lead* you to the *stately* tent of War,
> Where you shall heare the Scythian Tambur*laine*

and early in the first scene:

> Oft haue I heard your Maiestie com*plain,*
> Of Tambur*laine,* that sturdie Scythian thiefe,
> That robs your merchants of Persepolis,
> Treading by land vnto the Westerne Isles,
> And in your confines with his lawlesse *traine . . .*
>   (43-47)

---

16 See lines 284, 289, 293; 445. 446, 449, 450, 451, 453; 1010, 1013, 1015; 1313, 1315, 1318; 1664, 1666; 1728, 1729; 1916, 1917, 1920; 2152, 2153; 2196, 2197, 2198, 2200; 2584, 2585, 2586; 2985, 2989. 2993, 2994, 2995, 2997, 2998, 3000, 3001, 3004, 3005; 3009, 3010; 3103, 3108, 3110; 3223, 3226, 3228, 3232; 4593, 4594, 4597, 4598, 4602, 4603. Many of the Zenocrate echoes, e.g., several of those quoted above, carry associations of beauty and sublimity, thus adding to the atmosphere suggested by the name itself.

I quote some further examples:

> An vncouth *paine* torments my grieued soule,
> And death arrests the organe of my voice.
> Who entring at the *breach* thy sword hath *made,*
> Sackes euery *vaine* and artier of my heart,
> Bloody and in*sati*ate Tambur*lain.*
>> *Tam.* The thirst of *raigne* and sweetnes of a crown . . .
>
>   (858-863)
>
> So do we hope to *raign* in *A*sia,
> If Tambur*lain* be *plac'd* in Persea.
>
>   (889-890)
>
> Vntill I bring this sturdy Tambur*lain,*
> And all his Captains bound in captiue *chaines* . . .
>
>   (1212-3)
>
> So famous as is mighty Tambur*lain*:
> Shall so torment thee and that Callapine,
> That like a roguish runna*way,* suborn'd
> That villaine there, that *slaue,* that Turkish dog,
> To false his seruice to his Souer*aigne,*
> As ye shal curse the byrth of Tambur*laine.*
>> *Cal.* Raile not proud Scythian, I shall now reuenge
> My fathers vile abuses and mine owne.
>> *Ier.* By Mahomet he shal be tied in *chaines,*
> Rowing with Christians in a Brigandine,
> About the Grecian Isles to rob and spoile:
> And turne him to his *anc*ient *trade* a*gaine.*
> Me thinks the *slaue* should *make* a lusty theefe.
>> *Cal.* Nay, when the battaile ends, al we wil meet,
> And sit in councell to inuent some *paine,*
> That most may vex his body and his soule.
>
>   (3586-3601)

Such quotations could be produced almost indefinitely.[17] Certain echoing

---

17 For further obvious terminal echoes of Tamburlaine's name see also, e.g., the following sequences: *disdaine* (71), *Tamburlaine* (72), *Dame* (74), *away* (75), *day* (76), *Soueraigne* (78); *Tamburlaine* (239), *Swaines* (243); *traine* (282), *Tamburlaine* (286); *Tamburlaine* (553), *traine* (557), *Tamburlaine* (559), *plaines* (563); *Tamburlain* (1539), *remaine* (1543); *Danes* (2383), *Tamburlaine* (2384); *again* (2696) *Tamburlaine* (2698); *shame* (3136), *Tamburlaine* (3139), *sustaind* (3144), *meanes* (3145), *Tamburlain* (3148); *Tamburlaine* (3334), *runaway* (3339), *bay* (3341), *Soueraigne* (3343); *waues* (3514), *plaines* (3515), *Tamburlain* (3517); *streame* (3782), *againe* (3785), *Tamburlain* (3787); *Tamburlain* (3990), *tam'd* (3991); *Tamburlaine* (4154), *paines* (4158); *Tamburlaine* (4445) *paine* (4448). The number of instances of mere final assonance, showing little or no consonantal similarity with the last syllable of Tamburlaine's name, but often appearing in dense patterns. is great, as is also that of internal echoes, frequently rhyming, or nearly rhyming. Through such internal support, numerous final Tamburlaine echoes gain much in resonance.

expressions accompany Tamburlaine's name with particular frequency, e.g., *reign, chain(s), train, pain(s), great, state.* Their effectiveness in creating an appropriate atmosphere is obvious: they serve as it were as an extension of Tamburlaine's personality, both in sound and in substance. Allowing for some coincidence, one yet feels that coincidence alone could not possibly account for the persistence with which the theme of Tamburlaine saturates the play even phonetically.

In Marlowe's later works, the handling of phonetic effects follows essentially the same lines but seems less spectacular. He varies some of his procedures and often tones down his technique without attempting any striking new departures. But in *Tamburlaine* Marlowe is a genuine innovator, albeit an innovator whose methods are firmly rooted in a well, if not inspiringly, established tradition. The essential changes which he introduces are simple but effective. While his predecessors mostly liked a balanced distribution of echoes both at the line endings and in the middle of the lines, with some preference for the latter, Marlowe on the whole strongly shifts the emphasis toward the end of his iambic pentameters. The interior of the verse is thus disencumbered of emphasis. The line no longer falls into clearly marked sections but moves speedily towards its conclusion, on which the poet lavishes his most magnificent assonantal devices, often combined with the stately roll of dactylic polysyllables: hence much of their metallic or thunderous force. Literary influences may have played some part in this change. *The Spanish Tragedy* already has some of this shift of focus towards the end of the line, but it is exploited in a half-hearted fashion. Long terminal sequences of assonance occur in Seneca, the tragic model for most academically minded playwrights of the time.[18] Yet while Marlowe may be indebted to such precedents, the responsibility for the full, varied development of this terminal technique seems to be his own. At least equal originality is displayed in his thematic use of echoes, his manner of crowding them round some dominant theme—a name, a keyword, the ending of a refrain. By this method, the functional significance of his approach was enhanced, the music brought into more intimate association with the meaning, and the lyrical atmosphere strongly intensified. That there was much deliberation in his procedure seems established by

18 Seneca has numerous long successions of such echoes, e.g., in *Troades*: *ambiunt* (16), *domus* (17), *manus* (18), *obsitus* (20), *Illium* (22), *ferus* (23); *metus* (426), *malum* (427), *deus* (429), *specus* (430). *metus* (431), *exeunt* (432), *meum* (435), *metus* (437), *iugum* (439); *manu* (556), *hostilibus* (558), *manus* (533), *latus* (560), *locus* (562). See also any of the other plays, e.g., *Oedipus*: *caput* (532), *nemus* (533), *situ* (534), *latus* (535), *latus* (541), *ambitu* (543), *nemus* (544), *inscius* (545), *palus* (547), *gradum* (548), *locus* (549); *est* (274)_ *iacet* (275), *petens* (276), *iter* (277), *petens* (280), *biceps* (281); *videt* (204), *timens* (206), *iacent* (208), *timet* (209), *opem* (210), *edoce* (211), *iacent* (212), *licet* (215), *iubet* (218), *dies* (219); *fruit* (221), *coit* (224), *dedit* (227), *stetit* (229). Such passages abound in Seneca, and poets sensitized to assonance in their own language can hardly have helped noticing them.

such evidence as that of his assonantal "sonnets." But the effect even of
these sonnet-like structures, which seems so distinctive after being once
noticed, was probably on the subconscious rather than the conscious mind.
Marlowe's contemporaries are likely to have perceived such devices more
clearly than we do; but except for his fellow craftsmen in the field, even
they would hardly stop to trace assonantal arrangements with the intent-
ness that one might give to rhyme patterns. Actually, this seems to have
been one of the great advantages of this technique of overtones: it created
effects without the audience clearly realizing whence they derived. It stirred
up feeling without quite reaching the intellectual level: so, it was capable
of taking the listener unawares. It was thus exactly suited for achieving
that powerful lyricism which is perhaps Marlowe's greatest contribution
to English blank verse.

It may be assumed that Marlowe's new, brilliant methods of orchestration influenced Shakespeare's early blank verse, although comprehensive
studies would be needed to show to what extent. Shakespeare, after all,
was not just a continuator of Marlowe's work: he did not take up at all
points exactly where Marlowe left off. There were other playwrights to
learn from, whose procedures would have to be minutely examined before
drawing any definite conclusions as to the genealogy of Shakespeare's technical devices. Peele and Greene, for instance, seem to have been aware of
many of the effects obtainable by the use of echoing verse endings, but they
hardly approach Marlowe in the consistency or impressiveness of their
technique. (They resemble him in preferring final echoes to echoes inside
their lines but generally seem to have fewer of both.[19] Shakespeare's earliest
work is in this respect like theirs. Except for the dubious first part of
Henry VI, his internal assonances are seldom striking, and while final
assonance is not at all infrequent, it is less effective than that of Marlowe
at his best. The line, however, meeting with little internal phonetic and
pausal retardation, moves as easily to its conclusion as in Marlowe but
ends more rarely with equal flourishes of sound. It is, on the whole, closer
to *Edward II* than to *Tamburlaine.* Only somewhat later, and even then
by no means consistently, does Shakespeare really begin to exercise his
artistry in the handling of echoes. *Romeo and Juliet* contains a number of

---

19 There are, however, instances in Greene's *Orlando Furioso* where the polysyllabic,
    echoing style of *Tamburlaine* seems closely reproduced, e.g., in the grandiloquent speeches
    of the opening scene:
                  Erecting Statues of my Chiualry,
                  Such and so braue as neuer Hercules
                  Voud for the loue of louely Iole.
                  But leauing these such glories as they be,
                  I loue, my Lord; let that suffize for me.
                                          (Ed. J. Churton Collins, I.i.48-52)
    The last two lines, used as a refrain, form a leading motif which is echoed in the endings
    of at least two speeches. There are other refrain-like lines in this scene that are treated
    in the same way.

remarkable examples. The great love scenes, as well as some of the soliloquies, occasionally display a richness and subtlety in their sound-patterns that go beyond Marlowe. The word-plays in the lighter scenes (e.g. I.iv) seem inextricably embedded in echo series, which add to their resonance and complexity.[20] After having passed his apprenticeship in blank verse, Shakespeare is constantly apt to spring surprises on his readers in this as in other respects. Marlowe's virtuosity cannot have helped stimulating him, but less to direct imitation than to original effort. Less lyrical than Marlowe in *Tamburlaine,* more skilfully dramatic than Marlowe was even in his later plays, he seems to have varied his technique with great spontaneity as the occasion demanded. It is questionable, however, whether he could have done this so successfully without having been able to observe the impressive lengths to which the art of sound-arrangement had been carried by his highly gifted predecessor.

UNIVERSITY OF FLORIDA

---

20 For final echoes see, e.g., *R & J*, I.i.111 ff.: *abroach, began, adversary, approach, came, prepar'd, ears, winds, scorn, blows, part, part, to-day, fray, sun, East, abroad, sycamore, side, son = axbaxbbxaaccddedaaxe.* Note the striking correspondences *abroach, approach, sun, son.* The last, punning echo of this series occurs again in the next speech as part of another echo pattern: *sun, draw, bed, son, himself* (141-5) = *axbab.* The first thirty-nine line endings in scene IV of the same act are: *excuse, apology, prolixity, scarf, lath, crow-keeper, spoke, ent(e)rance, will, gone, ambling, light, dance, shoes, lead, move, wings, bound, shaft, bound, woe, sink, love, thing, rough, thorn, love, down, in, I, deformities, me, in, legs, heart, heels, phrase, on, done = xaabbxcbdcdxbexefgxgfxhfhxhxfxfifxxixjj.* But in this instance internal echoes, including punning homophones, play at least as important a part as the verse endings. Compare, e.g., lines 14-22:

    Rom. Not I, believe me. You have dancing *shoes*
With nimble *soles;* I have a *soul* of lead
So stakes me to the *ground* I cannot *move.*
    Mer. You are a *lover.* Borrow Cupid's *wings*
And *soar* with them *above* a common *bound.*
    Rom. I am too *sore* empierced with his shaft
To *soar* with his light feathers; and so *bound*
I cannot *bound* a pitch above dull *woe.*
Under love's heavy burden do I *sink.*

Such sequences as *ground, bound, bound, bound; soar, sore, soar, woe* combine punning with rhyme or assonance. The extremely intricate echo pattern, complicated by word-play, creates a rapid interaction of sound and meaning which is both slightly stunning and exciting. This scene is full of such light-hearted effects.

Music for the Replica Staging
of Shakespeare

by JOHN H. LONG

I N THE USUAL productions of Shakespeare's plays the music receives
scant consideration. This lack of attention is sometimes justified by
the nature of conventional stage practices. The use of the replica
stage, however, requires closer observation of the music, since music was
a stage device exploited fully not only by Shakespeare but by other
dramatists who wrote for the prototype of the replica stage.

In the past few years dramatic companies, both professional and amateur,
have experimented increasingly with the production of Shakespearean
plays on platform-type stages similar to those for which the plays were
written. The theory is that the closer the production can reproduce the stage
and other physical structures for which the plays were originally composed,
the more vitality and significance the plays will gain, and the simpler and
more effective the staging will be. This theory is of practical value only
up to a certain point—the point at which, to carry the idea to its logical
conclusion, it becomes necessary to reproduce the Elizabethan audience.
Before this point is reached, however, the production of Shakespeare's
plays can be, and seemingly is being, improved by replica staging. The
poetry, for example, takes on added significance when it replaces the scen-
ery to which we are accustomed. Likewise, the excision of act and scene
intervals in favor of continuous action adds momentum and increased
emotional impact to tue play as a whole.

It would be logical to assume, then, that if factors other than the physical
stage of the Elizabethans were studied and the result applied according to
the replica theory, the production would become even more effective. One
of these factors is the music called for by the plays. If the music and its
performance could be reconstructed and its dramatic functions studied
and the practices thus observed applied, it seems plausible that replica
staging would gain increased depth and unity. Indeed, the producer of
a replica stage play would save himself many headaches if he would give
due consideration to the music in his play.

The usual practices are that the producer either omits the scenes requiring music or that he uses music especially composed for his production.
Occasionally he will attempt to give an Elizabethan flavor to his perform-

ance by using old English music. None of these practices is efficient or artistic when applied to the replica stage. To avoid the problem of the music by omitting it is not fair to Shakespeare, who usually had a very good reason for using the music called for; nor is it fair to the producer, who might otherwise profitably use the music if he knew why it was originally employed; nor is it fair to the audience, which is deprived of its just due. To use modern music is to disturb aesthetic as well as dramatic unity. An imaginary, but valid, parallel to this practice would be the playing of a Stravinsky score on a harpsichord as incidental music for a medieval mystery play. And to use Elizabethan music, unless its nature and function in each case be understood, is to risk confusing the actors and the audience.

These statements are not intended as aspersions on the artistry or industry of producers as a group. They will retort, quite correctly, that even if they desire to use the type of music Shakespeare called for and which the replica stage requires, they have only vague and generalized information available on the use of music in the Elizabethan drama; that the scholarly research which is the basis of replica staging has not yet concerned itself seriously with the part played by music in Shakespeare's plays. Futhermore, they will add, little is known about the dramatic music of the period and about the instruments employed in the playhouses, nor has more than a handful of scores of a theatrical nature survived. Even if the music were available and its dramatic uses understood, they might conclude, there is great doubt that it would have much intrinsic value for the modern audience.

The writer has made a serious effort over the past several years to determine the part played by the music in Shakespeare's plays. So far, only ten of his plays have been studied. The project attempts to determine the dramatic function of each piece of music performed in the plays, to reconstruct the staging of each episode, to supply the musical scores used in each case or an appropriate substitute, and to draw some general conclusions regarding Shakespeare's dramatic technique. The work was founded on a study of the dramatic conventions of the period regarding the use of music, a study of Elizabethan music both vocal and instrumental, a close reading of Shakespeare's text, and a still-continuing search for appropriate Elizabethan scores.

One general conclusion early emerged. Shakespeare frequently used music to overcome the limitations imposed on him by the Elizabethan stage. To mention a few obvious examples: he calls for music to cover the noise made by clumsy machinery of the "lift" in *The Tempest*, IV. i; he draws nonexistent curtains at the end of *A Midsummer Night's Dream*

with music and dancing; he enlarges his stage with off-stage music suggesting an adjoining ballroom in *Much Ado,* I.i and ii. By observing the
technique with which Shakespeare used music to solve his problems of
staging, the modern producer on the replica stage should be able to solve
many of his problems in the same way. To be specific, suppose we reconstruct the serenade scene, IV.ii, of *Two Gentlemen of Verona.* Since my
reconstruction involves the performance of two pieces of music rather than
just one, as most editors of Shakespeare have it, and since I place the
performance of music off-stage in disagreement with almost all editors,
suppose we consider the whole scene closely.

The situation will be remembered as this: Julia, disguised as a boy, is
brought to the residence of Silvia by the Host of the inn where she is
staying in order that she might see her lover. She discovers Proteus serenading Silvia. The discovery and its effect on Julia are the dramatic focus
of the scene.

The question which Shakespeare faced at this point was this: How
could Julia show her grief without revealing her true identity to the Host?
His solution was to have the music performed associated by word-play
with Proteus. Such word-play, to be most effective, should be made while
the music is being performed. The question then arose, how could the
scene be staged so that the music would be prominent enough to assure its
association with Proteus and yet not interfere with the clear delivery of the
word-play which is the heart of the scene? I think he found the solution
in his source—a solution which permitted the song "Who is Silvia?" to be
sung without interruption and which provided an additional piece of instrumental music as background for the word-play.

In Montemayor's *Diana Enamorada,* the generally accepted source of
the play, Felismena, arriving at the city in search of her lover, takes
lodging at an inn. Late in the night she is awakened by the inn-keeper,
who tells her of a serenade to be performed in the street before the inn.
She opens her window and sees a group of musicians below. The music
begins with a piece played by three cornets and a sackbut. After the instrumental number, Don Felis, her lover, sings a song to the accompaniment
of a "dulcayna" and a harp. The initial pleasure of Felismena changes
to despairing grief when she realizes that Don Felis is not serenading her,
but another lady in the adjoining building.

In the play, Shakespeare of course ·retained the song, since it is the
occasion for the scene, but apparently he also retained the instrumental
music, placing it after instead of before the song as in Montemayor's story.
The song hence provides for Julia's discovery of Proteus, and the instrumental music provides the means by which Julia can express her reactions

to the discovery. Good stage practice suggests that the presence of the musicians on the stage and their playing would detract attention from the lines spoken by Julia and the Host while the music is sounding—lines that must be clear to the audience. The obvious solution is to move the musicians off-stage.

In the light of the foregoing statements, how would we reconstruct the staging of the scene? For our stage we need only a platform backed by a wall having three doors equally spaced across the stage. Since so little is known of the stages of The Theater, The Curtain, and The Rose playhouses, this arrangement is suggested as a common denominator of the three stages. It also agrees with the stage as seen by Quiller-Couch and Dover Wilson in the New Cambridge edition.

The setting is near Silvia's apartment in the Duke's palace. The left door represents a corner of Silvia's residence and also the path leading to the city and to the Host's inn. The center door represents an entrance to Silvia's apartment. The right door is another corner of the palace and also a path leading to another side of the palace.

The time is midnight.

Proteus enters through the left door as though coming from the city. Carrying a lute, he advances to the center of the stage. He speaks a short soliloquy, concluding:

"But here comes Thurio; now must we to her window,
  And give some evening Musique to her eare."

Thurio and three or four musicians enter from the left door as though also coming from the city. It will be remembered that, at the conclusion of III.ii, Thurio had promised to obtain musicians from the city for the serenade.

Th. How now, sir Protheus, are you crept before us.

Pro. I gentle Thurio, for you know that love will creep in service, where it cannot goe.

Th. I, but I hope, Sir, that you love not here.

Pro. Sir, but I doe: or else I would be hence.

Th. Who, Silvia?

Pro. I, Silvia, for your sake.

Th. I thank you for your own:

Proteus, Thurio and the musicians begin leaving the stage. Thurio continues speaking as they withdraw through the right door.

"Now Gentlemen? Let's tune: and too it lustily a while."

The serenaders have no dialogue assigned them until about forty-eight lines after this point. As they disappear, the Host and Julia enter through the left door as though coming from the city. Julia is disguised as a boy.

Ho. Now, my young guest; me thinks your 'allycholly; I pray you why
    is it?

Iu. Marry (mine Host) because I cannot be merry.

Ho. Come, we'll have you merry: ile bring you where you shall heare
    Musique, and see the Gentlemen that you asked for.

Iu. But shall I heare him speak.

Ho. I that you shall.

Iu. That will be Musique.

The Host and Julia walk across the stage while they talk. As they near
the right door, they hear musical instruments being tuned off-stage. Moving
to one side of the door, they look off-stage.

Iu. Is he among these?

Ho. I: but peace, let's heare 'em.

Proteus then sings "Who is Silvia?" As the song is performed, Julia dis-
plays signs of grief. At the end of the song the musicians stop playing
for a short while. The Host speaks:

Ho. How now? Are you sadder than you were before; how doe you,
    man? The Musicke likes you not.

Iu. You mistake: the Musitian likes me not.

Ho. Why, my pretty youth?

Iu. He plaies false (father.)

Ho. How, out of tune on the strings.

Iu. Not so: but yet so false that he grieves my very heart-strings.

Ho. You have a quick eare,

Iu. I, would I were deafe; it makes me have a slow heart.

Ho. I perceive you delight not in Musique.

Iu. Not a whit, when it iars so.

About this point, the musicians begin to play the instrumental piece,
probably a light dance tune which would contrast with the sweetly lyrical
nature of the song setting. The Host notices the difference in the music
being played.

Ho. Harke, what fine change is in the Musique.

Iu. I: that change is the spight.

The Host and Julia converse for a few more lines. The music ends.

Iu. Peace, stand aside, the company parts.

Julia and the Host move back against the wall at one side of the right door.
The serenaders enter through the same door, seemingly in the midst of
conversation.

Pro. Sir Thurio, feare not you, I will so pleade, that you shall say, my
    cunning drift excels.

Thurio then says farewell and leaves through the left door. Proteus and the musicians reach center stage. Silvia appears either at the center door or at a balcony.

Pro. Madam: good ev'n to your Ladiship.

Sil. I thanke you for your Musique (Gentlemen)
  Who is that that spake?

After bowing to Silvia, the musicians leave through the left door. Proteus and Silvia speak several lines, then Silvia withdraws and Proteus departs through the left door. Julia and the Host speak a few lines then leave the stage, also through the left door. The stage is now bare for the next scene.

By this disposition of dialogue, action, and music the scene is effectively fitted to the replica stage. The clear delivery of the word-play which is the focus of the scene is aided by placing it against a background of instrumental music rather than vocal music which would confuse the delivery of the lines. All dialogue ceases during the singing of the song; the intrinsic value of the song is thus enhanced. The effect of Julia's discovery is graphically portrayed by the frivolous music contrasted with her poignant comments. This staging is thus not only practical for the replica stage, but may well have been the arrangement used on Shakespeare's stage.

So far we have noted how a study of the music and its staging may solve production problems arising from the use of the replica stage. But what about the music itself, and its performance? The theory supporting replica staging would suggest that Elizabethan music might well be used on the replica stage. Two serious objections immediately will come to mind. Where may such music be found? And, if found, would it appeal to twentieth century tastes?

Elizabethan music of the proper type is generally available now, thanks to recent scholarly effort. The availability of the music, however, does not always solve problems pertaining to specific episodes in the plays of the period—particularly those of Shakespeare. The scene just considered will illustrate how both primroses and pitfalls may be encountered in supplying the early music for a Shakespearean play.

An instrumental score for the light dance music following Proteus' song can be found in almost any collection of Elizabethan music. Not the exact score that was originally used, mind, for there are no means of discovering it. The general type can be discovered, though. Of the several popular Elizabethan dances, the coranto, the jig, and the lavolta were the most light-hearted and active. For practical purposes, any one of these dances would be appropriate as an ironic contrast to Julia's emotions, and would also be different enough from the song accompaniment to be noticed by the audience as well as by the Host.

The setting for "Who is Silvia?" cannot be realized so easily. Here we find a pitfall. Whereas the folk-type songs of Shakespeare's day can be, and frequently were, set to several simple tunes interchangeably, the music for this particular song was most probably written especially for Shakespeare's lyric and for no other. Since the original music is lost, no surviving melodies are likely to fit the words exactly. The modern producer must then use a later setting, perhaps the one by Schubert, or have one composed for the occasion.

Assuming that the producer has the early music available and that he uses it, what guarantee has he that the modern audience will find it pleasing and appropriate? In the past, attempts have been made to use the early music without any notable degree of success. This result stems, I believe, from the lack of information regarding the types of music used originally, and from its method of performance, not from any serious incompatibility between the music and present audiences.

It seems to be a truism that the simpler and more tuneful a piece of music is, the longer it will remain current. Like good jokes, good tunes never die. Conversely, the more artistic is a piece of music, the closer it is associated with its historical period. As the later comprehension of that period dims, so fade the general understanding and appreciation of its reflection in music and other arts. Few now are interested by Lodge's euphuistic style or in listening to Morley's motets and madrigals, as lovely as some of us consider them. But the jokes that tickled the groundlings are still common fare, and the tunes to which these same groundlings set their ballads are still heard in many churches and in Tin Pan Alley.

The types of music most frequently used in the Elizabethan playhouses are those which we would class as folk music, popular music and semi-classical music. In Shakespeare's time the folk music would include traditional airs such as Desdemona's "Willow Song," and tunes used for rustic dances such as the morris and the hey. The popular music included the tunes, frequently of folk origin, set to ballads and broadsides, and the dance tunes used for the more urbane dances such as the galliard, coranto and lavolta. The semi-classical music would include the lutenist "ayres" and the dance music used for the more stately dances such as the pavane or the measure. Other types—the motets and madrigals, for example—were almost never used for dramatic purposes.

All of the types used on the stage are characterized by strong melodic content and marked rhythms—perhaps the marks of popular music in all ages. The lutenist "ayres" were usually art songs, that is, literate poetry set to a musical accompaniment especially composed by a skillful musician such as John Dowland, Thomas Morley or Francis Pilkington. While this type often showed a high degree of artistry, it usually had a single melody supported by a progression of chords—a simple structure when compared to the intricate polyphonic structure of the masses, motets and madrigals of the same period. In the lutenist ayres we find the beginning of the harmonic structure which we use now.

The point is this: if the producer of a Shakespeare play will limit the types of music he uses to those historically used in the plays, the chances are excellent that his audience will find the music as tuneful and appropriate as the music written for the latest Broadway revue, and frequently more musical.

The performance of the music is not a difficult matter. The ayres require vocalists with a fair degree of skill, but the folk songs may be, and in most cases should be, sung by untrained voices. Few producers should have trouble finding singers capable of performing the vocal music of Elizabethan plays.

The instrumental music requires more consideration. Ideally, its performance should be done on the musical instruments of the period because the music sounds to better advantage when played on them. In practice, this is almost an impossibility; there are few of these instruments outside of museums, and fewer musicians who can play them. The tonal qualities of the old instruments, however, can be simulated, often quite successfully, by making slight modifications on modern instruments. As a last resort, the music may be performed on modern instruments as they are.

When the producer selects a replica stage for his production of Shakespeare he automatically assumes a complex of historical problems. The type of stage used cannot be isolated from the action taking place on that stage, nor from other factors of production, such as the music, pertaining to that stage. To insist that the producer use Elizabethan musical instruments would be a *reductio ad absurdum,* but, frequently, the closer that we can approach the absurd without crossing the line, the more practical value has the theory. A careful consideration and application of Shakespeare's use of music to the modern versions of the Renaissance stage will often solve many problems before the producer becomes aware of them —problems which have already been considered and overcome by a man thoroughly familiar with the Elizabethan stage, William Shakespeare himself.

MOREHEAD STATE COLLEGE

Julius Caesar—a Morality of Respublica

by JOHN EARLE UHLER

CONCERNING Shakespeare's *The Tragedie of Julius Caesar*, or *The Life and Death of Julius Caesar*,[1] the tradition is almost entirely in favor of Brutus. He is interpreted as gentle, noble, and pure; whereas Caesar is seen to be physically infirm, superstitious, vacillating, pompous, and arrogant—written "down," as George Bernard Shaw says, so that Brutus might be written "up."[2] Brutus is therefore observed as the chief character of the play. Innes and others consider Brutus to be the hero.[3] Dowden, who epitomizes this view, writes that here Shakespeare "makes a complete imaginative study of the case of a man predestined to failure."[4] Hardin Craig too (and when Professor Craig speaks, Shakespearean students listen with admiration and respect), although he recognizes the play as mainly "of Caesar's revenge," writes that *"Julius Caesar* is a complete play of Brutus."[5]

Any effort to alter this view has the disadvantage, not only of tradition, but of the libel against a glorified literary character and of the necessity for establishing another view that carries more conviction and satisfaction. It is a disadvantage all the more onerous if the different view runs counter to the political mood of the present day. Since the trend of current politics is toward leftist democracy, such recent productions of *Julius Caesar* as those of Orson Welles and Margaret Webster have been encouraged in their anti-fascist complexion. Even an attitude of neutrality is likely to raise the hackles of Shakespearean criticism.

If, however, Shakespeare did not intend to glorify Brutus—if the proposition of his play is different from that generally interpreted since Hazlitt,[6] then it is a duty to search for the deeper meaning. In this search, one finds a few leads, first about Brutus, even among standard critics. To the opinion that Brutus' designs are "pure and noble," Ulrici adds a reservation,

---

1 In the First Folio at the beginning of the text the title is *The Tragedie of Julius Caesar*, but in the table of contents it is *The Life and Death of Julius Caesar*.
2 George Bernard Shaw, *Three Plays for Puritans* (New York, 1906) p. xxx.
3 *Julius Caesar*, ed. Arthur D. Innes (Boston, 1895), p. 11. Also see Hazelton Spencer, *The Art and Life of William Shakespeare* (New York, 1940) p. 223.
4 Edward Dowden, *Shakespeare; A Critical Study of his Mind and Art*, 3 ed. (New York, 1881), p. 249.
5 Hardin Craig *The Complete Works of Shakespeare* (Chicago, 1951). p. 772.
6 William Hazlitt, *Characters of Shakespeare's Plays* (London, 1917), pp. 26 ff. Of eighteenth century critics, who generally have little to say about Shakespeare's characters. as early an editor as Nicholas Rowe refers to "the virtue and philosophical temper of Brutus."

"apparently at least."[7]Hudson calls Brutus "a shallow idealist."[8] Hazelton Spencer observes that "there is more than a hint of the stuffed shirt about him."[9]

As for Spencer's opinion that Shakespeare "seems not quite certain what to make of Brutus,"[9] it is rather Spencer—usually quite discerning—who is uncertain. True, Brutus is regarded by different persons in the play in different ways. In any case, it must be conceded that he is highly respected in the community; he "sits high in all the people's hearts."[10] But a true guide for the judgment of character is not so much the opinion of "people" as it is the thought, word, and deed of the man himself. If we take the play scene by scene, it will be noted that Brutus' high seat in the people's hearts may be due, not only to his birth and social position, but to the front he puts up. It is chiefly he himself who is vocal in his own praise. It is he who says, "I love the name honor" (I.ii.88) and "I am arm'd so strong in honesty" (IV.iii.67) and "I can raise no money by vile means" (IV.iii.71). But the lean Cassius, who "looks quite through the deeds of men"(I.ii.102), and through their words too, observes, in soliloquy:

Well, Brutus, thou art noble; yet, I see,
Thy honorable metal may be wrought
From that it is dispos'd. (I.ii.312)

And he says to Brutus directly, "This sober form of yours hides wrongs" (IV.ii.40).

With more than ordinary caution, therefore, we examine Brutus' soliloquies at the beginning of Act II. Here, in passing, a word should be said about the dramatic function of the boy Lucius, a creation of Shakespeare's, not Plutarch's. Lucius is not, as is generally considered, a mere technical supernumerary, to fill up gaps in Brutus' action or to feed him substance for his lines. Lucius serves a far more important purpose; he is a direct foil to his master. Once in the conspiracy, Brutus cannot sleep (II.i.62). As Portia complains, he steals "out of his wholesome bed, / to dare the vile contagion of the night" (II.i.264); whereas the boy, in his innocence, enjoys "The honey-heavy dew of slumber" (II.i.230). He must be awakened at the beginning of the scene and, having ushered in the sinister midnight visitors whose "hats are pluck'd about their ears, / and half their faces buried in their cloaks" (II.i.74), he is not disquieted, or even curious; he drops off to sleep again. Even as he plays music for his master on the eve of battle, although he has slept "already" (IV.iii.263),

7 Hermann Ulrici, *Uber Shakespeares Dramatische Kunst,* in English tr. (London, 1847), p. 536.
8 Henry N. Hudson, *Shakespeare: His Life, Art, and Characters,* 4 ed. (Boston, 1872), II, 239.
9 Hazelton Spencer, *The Art and Life of William Shakespeare* (New York, 1940), p. 229.
10 *JC,* I. iii. 157. All references to Shakespeare's plays are to the Hardin Craig edition (op. cit), which in general follows the text of the Globe edition.

he dozes over his instrument at the risk of its injury (IV.iii.271). He pro-
vokes Brutus to say in envy, "I would it were my fault to sleep so soundly"
(II.i.4).

After rousing Lucius (first lines of Act II) and ordering him to light the
study, Brutus speaks his first soliloquy, to the effect that, although as yet
"the quarrel will bear no color for the thing" (II.i.28) that Caesar is, nevertheless Caesar should be thought "as a serpent's egg, / which hatch'd would
. . . grow mischievous," and therefore should be killed "in the shell"
(II.i.32).

Uncertain of the date, Brutus is informed by Lucius that "March is
wasted fifteen days," and he begins his third soliloquy, about his insomnia
(II.i.61). His "state"—the microcosm— "like to a little kingdom, suffers
. . . / the nature of an insurrection" (II.i.67), just as the macrocosm,
described by the frightened Casca (I.iii) is disturbed by a "civil strife in
heaven" (I.iii.11). After the third monolog, when Lucius announces the
conspirators, Brutus begins his fourth soliloquy about the shame of conspiracy, with its "monstrous visage" (II.i.81). In brief, as is revealed by
these very thoughts, (1) he does not recognize his enterprise as soundly
warranted; (2) he is distressed in mind; (3) he realizes that conspiracy is
hideous.

In this distraction he meets his fellow conspirators. He objects to an
oath of secrecy, with a grandiloquent assurance (twenty-seven lines) that
they need no "other bond / than secret Romans that have spoke their
word" (II.i.124), although, soon afterward, he betrays the secret to his
wife (II.i.305). He objects also to the assassination of Antony with an
equally grandiloquent preachment that the conspirators must appear not as
murderers but "purgers"—twenty-two lines vitiated at last with a two-line
anticlimax in contempt of Antony: "For he can do no more than Caesar's
arm / when Caesar's head is off," too ineffective to worry about: "Think
not of him" (II.i.162ff).

And, since the husband is partly known by his wife, Portia must not be
ignored in this consideration of Brutus. After appeals (II.i.237), fully as
turgid as her husband's, in which, on her knees, she begs for his secret, she
tells, as a "proof of my constancy," of the "voluntary wound" that she has
given herself in the thigh (II.i.300). For the neurosis behind such self-
mutilation, psychiatrists must have a word. Her act conforms with her hys-
teria a few hours later when she sends Lucius to the Capitol without an
errand (II.iv). She even fears that she has revealed the secret to the boy,
and she tries to cover up: "Brutus hath a suit, / that Caesar will not grant"
(II.iv.42). More in conformity with her self-infliction and at variance
with her constancy is her suicide on the eve of her husband's greatest trial,
before the battle of Philippi (IV.iii.156). Compare her with the resolute

Voluminia, or even the silent Virgilia, of *Coriolanus*—republicans of the earliest period, not the latest.

At the time of the assassination, it is Brutus, the leader, who is apparently the last to strike (III.i.76 and III.ii.190). Then he thinks of the dramatization of his act in ages hence (III.i.114). He refers to Antony, whom he has just condemned for his sports, wildness, and much company (II.i.188), as "a wise and valiant Roman; I never thought him worse" (III.i.138). Then after his brief speech to the people, he flees Italy. We next find him in a camp near Sardis, in a quarrel with Cassius, whom he charges with dishonesty (IV.ii and iii). Cassius, he says, is condemned to have "an itching palm" (IV.iii.10) and contaminates his fingers "with base bribes" (IV.iii.24). As for himself, Brutus declares, "I am so strong in honesty" (IV.iii.67) and "I can raise no money by vile means" (IV.iii.71), but he demands a share of the "vile trash" that he accuses Cassius of wringing from "the hard hands of peasants" (IV.iii.74). He upbraids Cassius: "I did send to you / for certain sums of gold, which you denied me" (IV.iii.69)—money for his legions (IV.iii.76), he says; but, regardless of its use or taint, he wants it. Furthermore, throughout the quarrel over this booty, it is Brutus who is violent, not Cassius. Beginning with a suggestion of chastisement, Brutus does most of the talking: "Let me tell you" (IV.iii.9) and "Hear me, for I will speak" (IV.iii.38). It can well be interpreted as a loud speech with accusations and exclamations and rhetorical questions, waxing in violence; whereas Cassius, with a few attempts at self-defence, falls back on quiet expressions of perplexity: "Is't possible?" (IV.iii.37)—"Must I endure all this?" (IV.iii.41)—"Is it come to this?" (IV.iii.50). And he yields to Brutus here, as always, by offering Brutus his dagger and his naked breast. "I, that denied thee gold," he says, "will give my heart" (IV.iii.104).

Before Brutus retires that night, he is visited by "Caesar's ghost," Brutus' "evil spirit" (IV.iii.275 and 282). In North's Plutarch, it is Brutus' "evil spirit,"[11] but not "Caesar's ghost"—apparently a Nemesis in either instance but, in Shakespeare, definitely related to Caesar, who seems to pursue Brutus to his death.

After the parley with Antony and Octavius, the two remaining conspirators speak of their possible defeat and their consequent destiny. Brutus says that, by the rule of his Stoic philosophy, he blamed Cato (Portia's father) for committing suicide. In the face even of Portia's suicide, the news of which has just reached him, he finds it "cowardly and vile, / for fear of what might fall, so to prevent / the time of life" (V.i.104). Here is

---

11 *Shakespeare's Plutarch*, ed. C. F. Tucker Brooke, (New York, 1909), I, 163. Unless otherwise stated all references to Plutarch are to Tucker Brooke's edition. "The horrible vision of a man" is Brutus' "ill angel" (p. 107).

another change that Shakespeare makes from Plutarch. In Plutarch, Brutus says that, although he did once blame Cato, now he is "of a contrary mind" . . . and will rid me of this miserable world" (p.170). By the change, Shakespeare very directly puts a blot of shame on the last act of both wife and husband.

What now of Antony's eulogy of Brutus at the end of the play: "This was the noblest Roman of them all" (V.v.68)? This praise is at variance with Antony's previous opinions. After the assassination, he had referred to Brutus as "butcher" (III.i.255), and, just before the battle, as "villain," "ape," "hound," "bondman," "cur," "flatterer"(V.i.39). After Brutus' death, in the light of such epithets, the praise is no more than that of the conventional funeral oration. Brutus had spoken words of the same sound over fallen Cassius, "the last of all the Romans. . . It is impossible that ever Rome should breed thy fellow" (V.iii.99). Over the bodies of Antony and Cleopatra, their enemy Octavius said, "No grave upon the earth shall clip in it / a pair so famous" (A&C,V.ii.362). Tullus Aufidius said of Coriolanus, "Though in this city he / hath widow'd and unchilded many a one / . . . yet he shall have a noble memory " (Coriolanus, V.vi.152). They are speeches of the conqueror over the conquered, after the formula aptly phrased by Prince Hal over the corpse of Hotspur:

> Thy ignominy sleep with thee in the grave,
> But not remember'd in thy epitaph!

If, then, we accept Brutus as Shakespeare intends him to be—not as we may subjectively read him into *Julius Caesar*—we cannot regard him as a tragic hero. Nor is Caesar so represented. The play is not a tragedy in the sense usually understood. This very fact has disturbed recent critics. Hazelton Spencer goes so far as to charge the work with "an absence of ideas." He writes, "If it is a play, and not an empty pageant, it is a political play," but unsurely he adds, "Shakespeare has little to say" about politics.[12] The editors of the brilliant Parrott edition make a statement somewhat similar, with a too nebulous addendum: "Shakespeare wrote *Julius Caesar* not to teach any political lesson, but to exhibit on the stage a great action and to give immortal life to the actors in that deed."[13] From the simple nineteenth century interpretation of the play as a drama of tyrannicide and tyranny's revenge, critics now begin to retire in uncertainty.

It is possible that certain further considerations will lead us more surely to the real meaning. In some respects the play is surprisingly in the mood of history contemporary with Shakespeare.Written in 1599, it appeared when Queen Elizabeth was sixty-seven years old, ill and almost imbecile. Her reign had been, under difficult circumstances, fairly strong and orderly, but

---

12 Op: cit., p. 229.
13 *Shakespeare*, ed. Thomas Marc Parrott *et al.* (New York, 1938), p. 633.

there was always a threat of assassination and the growing danger in the uncertainty of succession. Uncertainty might lead to anarchy, as in France, where the succession after Henry III, also childless, had been in doubt, and where "domestic fury and fierce civil strife" (*JC,* III.i.264) during the 1590's cumbered all the parts of the country. And England was in danger of a similar prospect by Elizabeth's death. The common people, moreover, had risen to such power that, within fifty years, they could and did arraign their king and execute him—and plunge the land into civil war. The imminence of a new order, with possible anarchy, was on the horizon.

Of this state of affairs Shakespeare was no doubt completely sensible. To its dramatization he was able to add a sound philosophy of politics. As is revealed in his English history plays—recently interpreted with consummate clarity by E. M. W. Tillyard[14]—Shakespeare dwelled heavily on the rights of succession, the virtue of political structure that tapered orderly to a head, the graces of the ideal monarch, and the evils of sedition. In the 1590's, Shakespeare was deeply engrossed in these aspects of *Respublica.*

As is also emphasized by Tillyard, the literature of Shakespeare's time abounded in allegories, of which *The Faerie Queene* is the foremost example, a poem political in tenor as well as moral. Allegorical plays about politics—some being pure moralities, others after the manner of moralities —were sufficiently numerous to effect a trend. Notable among earlier plays of this kind are *Respublica,* Skelton's *Magnificence,* Lyndsay's *Satire of the Three Estates,* and Bale's *King John.* In *Respublica* is the title character Respublica (the state), who is at first controlled by four persons, chiefly Avarice, who puts up a front and changes his name to Policy, replete with apparent ideals but narrow and selfish in action. Two other characters are People and Nemesis. The general meaning is expressed in the Prolog: common-wealths decay when Avarice, Flattery, Oppression, and Insolence "have the rule in their possession."[15] Of allegorical significance too—and of later creation—is *Gorboduc.* It is meant to teach that (1) anarchy results from uncertain royal succession; (2) order in the state is a corollary of order in nature, and

> . . . nature hath her order and her course,
> Which being broken doth corrupt the state
> Of mind and things; (I.ii.220)

(3) "though kings forget to govern as they ought, / yet subjects must obey as they are bound" (V.i.50); and (4) "right will always live and rise at length, / but wrong can never take deep root to last" (V.ii.278).

Historical-morality plays still later than *Gorboduc* are, among others, the *True Tragedy of Richard III,* with its prolog involving Truth and Poetry

14 *Shakespeare's History Plays* (New York, 1946), passim.
15 *Respublica,* ed. for E. E. T. S. by Leonard A. Magnus (London, 1905).

and Clarence's ghost, and Wilson's *Three Lords and Three Ladies of London,* in which the lords are Policy, Pomp, and Pleasure, and the ladies Love, Lucre, and Conscience. As the history plays continue, the too obvious allegory subsides, but a strong tinge of the morality remains. Of these later plays, the *True Tragedy of Richard III, Life and Death of Jack Straw,* and Heywood's *Edward IV* dwell heavily on the evils of conspiracy and rebellion. In Marlowe's *Edward II,* Canterbury says, "Lift not your swords against the king" (I.ii.61), and Kent, who violates the precept, later suffers remorse and laments the state "where lords keep courts and kings are lock'd in prison" (V.iii.63).

Shakespeare's plays about England's history follow the tradition, with the same lessons. Tillyard, among others, sees a clear morality design. About the first tetralogy, he says that it has no regular hero, "its true hero being England or Respublica after the fashion of the Morality Play,"[16] just as Knight says that "the hero of Shakespeare's classical trilogy is Rome."[17] Gervinus is close to this interpretation: "The poet has handled this historical piece like his English historical plays."[18] About the second tetralogy, Tillyard continues this idea. Samuel Daniel, in the *Civil Wars*—so writes Tillyard—"shares with Shakespeare the morality motive of Respublica when he makes an allegorical female figure, the Genius of England, reprove Bolingbroke."[19] Tillyard elaborates further in showing that Prince Hal is torn, "morality-fashion, between Sloth or Vanity, to which he is drawn by his bad companions, and Chivalry, to which he is drawn by his father and brothers."[20]

The projection of the English history plays into *Julius Caesar* is a fairly recent view. As has been noted, Gervinus intimates it. Parrott calls *Julius Caesar* a "link-play" between the histories and the great tragedies.[21] Campbell repeats the idea.[22] But no one has heretofore penetrated beyond these vague hints.

A suspicion that might provoke further search derives from the allegorical quality of various symbols in the play. The crown that is offered Caesar, as Casca explains, is not a crown, but "one of these coronets" (I.ii.237). Brutus loves the *name* of honor (I.ii.88); he has a noble *form* (IV.ii.40). When sleepless, he is contrasted with the emblem of sleep in Lucius. The notes that he thinks he receives from the people are but imitations of reality (I.ii.319). He is disturbed by the *appearance* of con-

---

16 Op. cit., p. 163.
17 Charles Knight, *Studies of Shakespeare* (London, 1851), p. 405.
18 G. G. Gervinus, *Shakespeare Commentaries,* tr. F. E. Bunnètt, 2 ed. (London, 1883), p. 721.
19 Op. cit., p. 240.
20 Ibid., p. 265.
21 Op. cit., p. 629.
22 Oscar J. Campbell, *The Living Shakespeare* (New York, 1949), p. 699.

spiracy (II.i.81). The first person to fall after Caesar is the poet Cinna, who is attacked only for his *name* (III.iii). And it is not Caesar that Brutus wishes to destroy, but Caesar's *spirit* (II.i.167); ironically it is Caesar that he does destroy. Caesar's spirit survives as a *nemesis* to plague Brutus to his defeat and death.

It is reasonable then to apply to the play of Roman history the same formula that Tillyard and others apply to the plays of English history, and it remains only to interpret *Julius Caesar* in accordance with that formula.

The interpretation is easier in the light of Roman politics. The republic, almost five hundred years old at the time of Caesar, was in decadence. Its plight is described by Appian, with whose history Shakespeare could have been acquainted. Appian is named in one of Thomas North's captions in Plutarch's "Life of Brutus" (p.188). In Appian—not in Plutarch—are speeches much like those that Shakespeare has Brutus and Antony make to the people.[23] It could well be, then, that Shakespeare knew the Greek historian's description of Rome in Caesar's day: "The government had been corrupt for a long time. The plebeians were now mixed with foreign blood, freedmen had equal rights of citizenship with them, and slaves were dressed in the same fashion as their masters . . . Moreover, the distribution of corn to the poor, which took place in Rome only, drew thither the lazy, the beggars, the vagrants of all Italy. The multitude of discharged soldiers" . . . secured "unjust allotments of lands and houses belonging to others."[24] Such riffraff (North calls them "rakehells of all sorts"[25]) made up the audience to whom Brutus and Antony spoke.

These are People, as in a morality play. They are not similar to People of *Respublica,* but to Jack Cade's followers in the Second Part of *Henry VI,* or to the people in *Coriolanus,* or to the "whores and knaves" in the commonwealth of the fatuous idealist Gonzalo of *The Tempest* (II.i.166). They are People without discipline—the shiftless hands and feet of the Commonwealth, as described in Menenius' fable in *Coriolanus* (I.99), the "mutable rank-scented many" (III.i.66), rank-scented in spirit as well as in body. And as the people are, so is the state likely to be.

After 49 B.C., after the Rubicon, the Roman state was Julius Caesar, "the foremost man," as Brutus admits, "of all this world (*JC,* IV.iii.22). Like Louis XIV, Caesar might have said, "L'état c'est moi." But the republic was in its last stages, with only vestiges of whatever force holds the body politic together, call it what you will: cooperation, order, direction, discipline, authority, or, in impending destruction, absolutism, which

23 *Roman History,* tr. Horace White (London, 1913), IV, 479 ff.
24 Ibid., IV, 451.
25 Plutarch, p. 135. Also see "The Life of Julius Caesar," p. 144: "The common people that had sold their voices for money came to the market place at the day of election, to fight for him that had hired them."

always dominates the transition to birth or death. Like Queen Elizabeth, Caesar was old, ill, and imbecile, with the "falling sickness" (I.ii.256). Like Elizabeth, he made up for his growing ineptitude by the bark of a dog which is losing its bite: "Always I am Caesar" (I.ii.212)—"Danger knows full well / that Caesar is more dangerous than he" (II.ii.44)—"Wilt thou lift up Olympus?" (III.i.74)—just as Elizabeth is reported to have said to Cecil before her death: "Is *must* a word to be addressed to princes?" —"Thou art so presumptuous because thou knowest I shall die"[26]

If Caesar is not the enfeebled Respublica, at least he represents one aspect of its senescence, the loss of command, just as People represents the loss of obedience. As Plutarch intimates, the one follows the other, and the result is so disastrous that tyranny may become expedient. He quotes Favonius' reply to Brutus to the effect that "civil war was worse than tyrannical government" (p.124). Plutarch's own opinion is that Rome was "now brought to that pass, that it could no more abide to be governed by many Lords, but required one absolute Governor" (p.182).

As in the morality, the central figure, Respublica, is torn between two forces, represented chiefly by Brutus and Antony. If Shakespeare writes Caesar "down" from Plutarch, he writes Brutus down also, as is shown in the changes made from Plutarch to the derogation of Brutus. Even Plutarch himself is unsure of his hero and sometimes contradicts himself. Although he represents Brutus as flattered by Cassius, who says to Brutus that the people do not seek entertainment from him (p.122), yet, later, Brutus is pictured as entertaining the people with free "games and sports," and "strange beasts" and "players" and "musicians" (p.140). In another passage, Plutarch describes Brutus as "marvellous lowly and gentle," never "in any rage" (p.151), yet Plutarch says that Brutus speaks to Casca "in choler" (p.179). With Cassius Brutus is "hot and loud," and thrusts his friend "out of the chamber," and calls him "dog, and counterfeit cynic" (pp.160-61). Although "merciful, just, and courteous"[27] he steals upon the Lycians "as they were at dinner, and slew six hundred of them."[28] In the "Life of Brutus," he is not "afraid" of the ghost (p.163), but in the "Life of Caesar," he is "marvellously afraid" (p.104). It is little wonder that actors interpret the part differently, as Colley Cibber notes in his *Apology*. Betterton played the part with "unruffled temper," although some other actors were as "warm as Hotspur."[29]

In view of all the evidence, although Brutus may be pictured as a man

26 John Richard Green, *Short History* (London, 1874), p. 459.
27 P. 157; also see p. 158.
28 P. 154; also see p. 178: "Now for the slaves that were prisoners . . . he commanded they should kill them. But for the freemen he sent them freely home."
29 *An Apology for the Life of Mr. Colley Cibber* (London, 1740), p. 87. Note that even Cibber is unsure of Betterton's interpretation.

of principle, yet he fails in practice. He may be considered the embodiment of Principle-without-Practice, a schizophrenic, "with himself at war" (*JC*,I.ii.46), a part of the chaos that was closing in on the sick Respublica. And, as ambivalent People breaks into a riot, so Principle-without-Practice, after having destroyed the only authority that, though weak, was keeping the state in any order at all, helps provoke a great civil war. The threat of tyranny is evil, but assassination (or call it tyrannicide) is no cure; it is rather of the general ill.

Antony, on the other hand, is built "up" from Plutarch. To be sure, he is represented as self-indulgent. Caesar says that he "revels long o' nights" (II.ii.116). Brutus says that "he is given to sports, to wildness, and much company" (II.i.188), but also that he is a "wise and valiant Roman" (III.i.138). After the assassination, he is pictured as a demagogue, but so is Brutus, who succeeds so well as to provoke "Let him be Caesar" (III.ii.56). Without any comment on Antony's virtues, like his fidelity to Caesar and his military skill and his support of Caesar's heir, which might tempt an interpretation setting him up as a morality-like virtue, Antony may be regarded, at the worst, as Practice-without-Principle. Through the play, he gives the impression of being chiefly a soldier, whereas Brutus is chiefly a politician. The dyarchy of the decadent Republic—the Senate and the Army—as depraved in their way as the people were in theirs, had split, one on one side of authority, or good order (or of Respublica), the other on the opposite side.

Politics inevitably puts up a front of principle, and its use to the commonwealth depends on the practice of that principle—and, in any case, on the prevalence of order. The military stresses practice over principle, because victory, by right or wrong, is its aim. Moreover, order is of the army's very essence. It is composed of a hierarchy, in which its lowest members have definite rank, and its very nature and function are to fight through disorder for the restoration of order. In a healthy commonwealth, in which politics puts its principles into wise practice, the military stands by for support. But if Respublica is senile and corrupt, and politics takes to contrivance (as it often does), then chaos is around the corner. It is such conditions that Plutarch describes in the "Life of Cicero."[30] The Age of Generals had come; they were the colossi, under whose legs the politicians walked and peeped about to find themselves dishonorable graves. Under such conditions, politics resorts to conspiracy and to the assassination of disabled Respublica, and then, plagued by the very ghost of the commonwealth, takes to flight. For the re-embodiment of Respublica, with a restored political order, the military steps in. So—whether we like

---

[30] "Life of Cicero," *Plutarch's Lives*, tr. John Dryden, rev. H. H. Clough (London, 1888), pp. 77 ff.

the Empire or not (and the question as such does not come up in *Julius Caesar*)—Antony helps Octavius, Caesar's legal heir, to his inheritance, and, so far as the play goes—and as Appian explains[31]—Antony, Octavius and Lepidus make themselves triumvirs for re-establishing the state.

Julius Caesar is therefore a tragedy, not of a person, Caesar or Brutus, but, morality-like, of Respublica. Respublica may drop from "the falling sickness" or from the chaotic impact of assassination, but its existence is proof against both. No idle boast, that: "Always I am Caesar" (*JC*,I.ii.-212). Though the king be dead, long live the king. As Menenius in *Coriolanus* says,

> . . . You may as well
> Strike at the heaven with your staves as lift them
> Against the Roman state, whose course will on
> The way it takes . . . (*Coriolanus*,I.i.69)

so Respublica, which "walks abroad" (*JC*,V.iii.95) in spirit during the chaos of civil war and turns the swords of the conspirators into their "own proper entrails" (V.iii.95), takes a new "course" (*Coriolanus*,I.i.71) in Octavius, who has the last word of the drama:

> So, call the field to rest, and let's away,
> To part the glories of this happy day.

LOUISIANA STATE UNIVERSITY

---

[31] Op. cit., IV, 373.

Dramatic Significance in *Hamlet*

by RICHARD PAUL JANARO

IT SEEMS to be generally accepted that Shakespeare and Montaigne went hand in hand a great deal of the time. We know that *Hamlet* is permeated with the thought of the French philosopher.[1] It is tempting to seek a consistent philosophic unity in the play; yet it is also enlightening to look further, to see what the Montaigne perspective implies when it is seen at work behind the dramaturgical precept in terms of which alone could *Hamlet* have been written.

A representative modern view of *Hamlet* is that of Professor Hardin Craig, who finds in the play the development of a stoic ideal, not passive inertia, but rather the desire to act, prompted by the conviction that one must ready himself to cease acting at any moment.

> It follows that, to achieve happiness, one might say victory, Hamlet, like all men, must control his mind. Control of mind is a goal of the Renaissance, reinforced by stoical teachings. The Renaissance knew that unhappiness ties man's hands and leaves him in impotent misery. Man must arrive at a point where he can calmly meet his fate, no matter what it is. He must be indifferent to consequences, but he must also act.[2]

This concept finds strong basis in Montaigne's

> I would have a man to be doing, and to prolong his lives offices, as much as lieth in him, and let death seize upon me, whilest I am setting my cabiges, carelesse of her dart, but more of my unperfect garden.[3]

Dr. Craig finds, moreover, that

> the course of Hamlet's struggle can be traced through the soliloquies and the dialogue to the point in the fifth act . . . where Hamlet gives expression to the ultimate significance of the play.[4]

He refers, of course, to the most pointedly stoic speech in the play: "If it be now, 'tis not to come; if it be not to come, it will be now; if it be not now, yet it will come: the readiness is all"[5].

---

1 See Alice Hammon, "How Great Was Shakespeare's Debt to Montaigne?" *PMLA*, LVII (1942), 988-1008; Elizabeth Hooker, "The Relation of Shakespeare to Montaigne," *PMLA*, XVII (1902), 312-366.
2 *An Interpretation of Shakespeare* (N.Y., 1948), p. 183.
3 *The Essayes of Michael Lord of Montaigne*, tr. Florio (London, 1908), I, 85.
4 Craig, op. cit., p. 187.
5 V.ii.231-34.

This could certainly be yet another echo of Montaigne:

> Moreover, no man dies before his houre. The time you leave behinde
> was no more yours than that which was before your birth, and con-
> cerneth you no more . . . Wheresoever your life endeth, there is it
> all . . . It consists not in number of years, but in your will, that you
> have lived long enough.[6]

Thus it is exceedingly probable that two minds of the same epoch gave
birth to parallel propositions. But the dramatic expression which Shakespeare gave to these and other popular ideas belongs to the Renaissance,
not to us. It is necessary to construct a clearer picture of dramaturgical
practice in Shakespeare's age. What technology with which we are familiar
could possibly, could conceivably have guided it? When we use a term
like *significance* with respect to the drama, we must remember that the
form itself is a linear one, different from all other media. Because it consists of a series of once-played scenes and once-spoken dialogues, because
we are at any given point exposed to but a single dramatic moment, the
total significance of a play must: a) reside in each moment as it comes; or
b) be cumulative, so that each scene bears within itself the meaning of all
that has gone before and directs the way toward what is to follow. In the
latter case, the "ultimate significance" of a play is to be found in the climax.
Hedda Gabler, for example, does not fully *mean* until Judge Brack's curtain
speech "Good God! People don't do such things!" has shown us the ironic
uselessness of Hedda's suicide.

In the case of Shakespeare we really cannot speak of "ultimate significance" at all. There is only a succession of moments or crises which may
or may not relate to one another, but which cannot be looked upon as
forming a developmental pattern. This is not to be judged immature drama-
turgy. It is simply a question of relative standards, of the only context of
dramatic theory in which it is possible to place Shakespeare.

The notion of "progress," of change in the drama is relatively modern.
What Montaigne lives in terms of is a static universe. This is the reason
that Montaigne can fortify himself against the certainty of death.

> And if you have lived one day, you have seene all: one day is equal
> to all other daies: There is no other light, there is no other night. This
> Sunne, this Moone, these Starres, and this disposition, is the very
> same, which your forefathers enjoyed, and which shall also entertaine
> your posteritie. [7]

We cannot safely assume that Elizabethan dramatists had no awareness of,
gave no thought to the phenomenon of character evolution or of cumu-

6 Florio, I, 93.
7 Ibid., I, 91.

lative significance. But we *can* assume that these would have been remarkable notions, unlikely to have been integral to the heritage of popular theatre practice.

Concerning the origin of the idea of and term for *evolution* as we understand it today, Mr. Logan Pearsall Smith writes:

> Evolution is, of course, a modern word in English; it appeared first in a military sense in the XVIIth century, and acquired its present meaning and its immense development from the works of Darwin and Herbert Spencer in the XIXth century.[8]

The notion of "progress" as we would conceive it with application to the drama, prior to the eighteenth century

> may have visited the thoughts of a few lonely philosophers, but it obtained no general acceptance, and found no expression in the language . . . Even at the Reformation, the ideal, as the word *Reformation* shows, was that of a return to the purity of primitive and uncorrupted times; and the conception of continuous evolution, of an advance beyond the limits set by the past, is one which appeared at a late period in the history of human thought.[9]

Now, if *Hamlet* is to have "ultimate significance," the concept cannot be disassociated from that of continuous evolution. When we consider the trial-and-error experimentalism of Elizabethan drama, it becomes still more difficult to attribute so revolutionary a principle to Shakespeare. We should have to grant him not only the thought but the transformation of that thought into a functional, continuously evolving dramatic structure.

Another concept that needs clarification is that of "character." The developmental pattern, if it existed at all in *Hamlet,* could be expected to reach its ultimate significance in terms of an adjustment in the hero's personality, in his subjective attitude towards life. But here again, when we say "character," we must first understand what is meant. Are we speaking of an agent in a dramatic situation? In this case "character" could change, but not necessarily develop, to meet the demands of situation. Or do we intend "character" as a pyschological abstraction? At the time of Shakespeare the notion of *self* was but dimly conceived. The terms *ego, egoism,* and *egotism* were first created by French philosophers in the seventeenth century and did not even appear in English until Addison used them.[10] And, though Montaigne's writings are really introspective, the term *consciousness* was not recognized in its now-accepted sense until Locke's definition appeared in 1632.[11] It is not too much to say that a

---

8 *The English Language* (N.Y., 1912), p. 224.
9 Ibid., p. 225.
10 Ibid., p. 236.
11 Ibid., p. 244.

symbol must be invented almost as soon as there is recognized need for it. The notion, then, of "self" as an abstraction was in the air in Shakespeare's day, but is it at all likely that the popular drama would have been concerned with it? Presently I shall make the assertion that there are internal as well as external struggles in *Hamlet,* but to say that Shakespeare found good dramatic stuff in the static opposition between a man's light and dark angels is not to say that Shakespeare knew anything of the relation between experience and the evolving ego. Internal and external alike are stretched out side by side on a one-dimensional plane of drama.

Thus, while our drama implies an identification of the hero through each progression, the hero in Elizabethan popular drama remains only nominally identifiable from scene to scene. And sometimes, with the enormous opportunity for variety offered by the convention of "disguise," even this identification was not essential. The moment is the only possible unit of measurement; so long as there was a hero in a situation, a focal point for the audience's sympathetic attachment, it mattered not whether hero one was identical with hero two. In this context what can "identical" possibly mean? What difference need it make? Audiences, carried along by the dazzling array of all possible dramatic involvements, have never been confused. To Hamlet—a *tabula rasa* played throughout by the same actor, the *given* protagonist who must defeat the king whatever shall befall—is ascribed a set of attributes for the immediate purposes of a given scene. Any change that appears to occur is, in reality, the substitution of one set of attributes for another. "Dramatic significance" in *Hamlet* becomes the emotional appreciation of these attributes at each moment in conflict with something that is beyond the control of the hero, something that is absolutely and statically set out of harmony with his well-being. The Montaigne darkness did influence the course of Elizabethan tragedy, but it was a darkness that had been there long before Montaigne's memorable definition. On the one hand, there was the sunny optimism which the notion of eternal order could imply; on the other, the image of eternal dissolution, the image of the tragic situation. But the moment was sufficient to itself. The passing of years, Montaigne observed, repeated the same story. Hamlet as hero has had a host of reasons for doing a host of deeds, but it is the time-marking action that matters in the end. Hamlet never becomes a symbol, an idea with an iota more of meaning than he had at the outset.

In the first truly dramatic situation—that is, when the Ghost informs him of the murder—Hamlet is shown us as an energetic, opportunistic youth.

Haste me to know't, that I, with wings as swift
As meditation or the thought of love,
May sweep to my revenge.[12]

He is an exemplary Renaissance hero, the master of the situation, the most likely prospect for a revenge plot. Without the least bit of meditation he plans his "antic disposition," possibly taking a hint from Horatio's "These are but wild and whirling words, my lord." This is the Hamlet who more or less acts as master of ceremonies, who keeps the "show" going. He has all the stock attributes for the man of action but no personality, in our sense, at all. It is he who knows what use to make of the players so soon as he sees them, since after all, the play within a play had already proved its merits as a prize dramatic device. It is he who can slay Polonius by mistake, dispose of the body without a qualm, who can with great deliberation write out the death warrant for Rosencrantz and Guildenstern and merely comment:

They are not near my conscience. Their defeat
Doth by their own insinuation grow.
'Tis dangerous when the baser nature comes
Between the pass and fell incensed points
Of mighty opposites.[13]

And it is this Hamlet who dies, this basic, changeless hero. Like Marlowe's heroes, he has lived on intimate terms with a world of violence and danger, has asserted his will, has killed and agreed to be killed. What troubles him finally is not the meaninglessness of life and man, but rather, his "wounded name."

Hamlet, the folk-hero, possesses in general both will and courage, the two virtues most likely to arouse the admiration of the audience. Suppose, however, he should from time to time be made to suspect himself of cowardice? Here was a likely invention whereby Shakespeare could, whenever he chose, delay the certain outcome: the victory, which alone could satisfy audience desires for security in an uncertain world. A forced delay would gratify the need for emotional stimulation, the strange pleasure of which has always sent people to the theatre. There is a Hamlet in the play who would reach the status of hero if he could. His ideal is set forth in his very first scene with Horatio when he describes his father:

He was a man, take him for all in all,
I shall not look upon his like again.[14]

In the second soliloquy Hamlet berates himself in these terms:

---

12 I.v.29-31.
13 V.ii.58-62.
14 I.ii.187-88.

'Swounds, I should take it; for it cannot be
But I am pidgeon-liver'd and lack gall
To make oppression bitter, or ere this
I should ha' fatted all the region kites
With this slave's offal.[15]

But note that Hamlet has little justification for this attitude, since he has
cleverly seized the first opportunity for action that has presented itself.
Picture an Elizabethan audience accepting for very long a man who did
not!

It can only be that the coward Hamlet constitutes a separate situation
that is not really introduced again until the fourth soliloquy. The dramatic
effectiveness of self-doubt on the part of the hero, immediately before the
final showdown, cannot be questioned, but we are not to assume that the
personality of the hero has been *developing* to this point.

There is another factor, suggested by Shakespeare: Hamlet's basic dislike
for his assignment.

The time is out of joint;—O cursed spite
That ever I was born to set it right![16]

This attitude has frequently been taken as a clue to the "pre-play" Hamlet,
and it is true that our very first impression of him is of a melancholy,
regressive introvert. Even the King points out this characteristic: "How is
it that the clouds still hang on you?" The word "still" has had unfortunate
reverberations. The obvious factor has frequently been ignored: that is,
Shakespeare sets up at once a sharp and absolute conflict between the two
"mighty forces." Hamlet is suspicious of his uncle from the first, for his
immediate reaction to the Ghost's revelation is, of course, "O my pro-
phetic soul!" Moreover, he exhibits unmistakable signs of relief following
his interview with the Ghost. Thus the Hamlet who appears to shun his
duty altogether is by no means integral to the action at any point, never
reappears again, and must be regarded as a separate creation. Perhaps,
significantly enough, Shakespeare saw too few possibilities in using as hero
one who would prefer not to surrender himself to action. It is quite
another matter to allow the hero to suffer *within* the confines of the active
situation. Here, on safer ground, all kinds of dramatic inventions would be
possible.

Thus Hamlet Four should not be looked upon as a stumbling block. It
is he who must "have grounds more relative than this." It is he who thinks
"too precisely on th' event," thus losing the "name of action." Yet this
Hamlet never suggests that the enterprise is not to his liking, nor is it a

15 II.ii.604-08.
16 I.v.189-90.

question of cowardice with regard to the dangerous game he must play. It is moral cowardice with which hero four has been identified, a certain tendency to upset the balance between action and thought. Here is a man who simply wastes time, an unpardonable sin for the Elizabethans, a great suspense-provoking factor. All through the plays of the period one notes a preoccupation with the theme of Time, a villain that was certain to be outwitted. To be, like Hamlet, pressed for time, to pause now and then, just when pause could be disastrous, and yet to succeed at last—here was a wish-fulfillment of major proportions for Shakespeare's audience. Nor is this situation, as an independent dramatic device, so prevalent as we might suppose. Hamlet gives his desire for certainty as an excuse for the play-within-a-play, but, after all, it was the big scene that mattered.

The first real indication that Hamlet's meditations interfere with action occurs in the "To be or not to be" soliloquy, the subject matter of which bears no relation whatever to its context. Moreover, the "action" discussed is suicide and not the murder of the King. Fancy the Elizabethans showing serious concern lest their hero do away with himself mid-way through the play! Professor E. E. Stoll has made a very fine suggestion for the significance of the speech when he mentions the "anxiety in the audience lest, as he (Hamlet) comes in ruminating, he should betray himself."[17] This would mean that *any* sort of contrivance would be dramatically acceptable under the circumstances. Sensitive staging of this scene would emphasize the eavesdroppers rather than the "meaning" of the words that Hamlet speaks! We note further that, even when his introversion is alluded to by Hamlet, there is never a situation to serve as evidence, never an instance in which his inability to act becomes dramatically important. There are time-wasting scenes, suspense scenes, but at the moments of crisis, when pure action is called for, Hamlet is the folk-hero. The "prayer scene" is a good example of the use to which Shakespeare puts hero four. Hamlet's speech requires time at a dangerous moment, and it points the way toward the more exciting showdown to come. Hamlet's reasons for not killing the King, moreover, have nothing whatever to do with his self-reproaches for over-scrupulous meditation.

The next reference to procrastination is by the Ghost in his reappearance during the "closet" scene. But here again our focus should be upon the dramatic purpose served by the second use of the supernatural, rather than upon the specific content of the Ghost's speech. The "blunted purpose" would, again, be merely a slight motivation for the device itself. Hamlet apologizes for being "laps'd in time and passion," but, coming as it does on the heels of the play scene, the speech lacks immediate reference.

---

17 *Hamlet the Man*, English Association Pamphlet No. 91 (March, 1935), p. 19.

The final appearance of the "theme" is in the last soliloquy. It is surprising to note, however, that Hamlet does not refer at all to his having failed to kill the King—a staggering omission for so meticulous a hero! Again the speech is a time-consuming factor and serves a dramatic function unrelated to its content. It comes immediately after the King has announced his plans to have Hamlet killed in England. Hamlet's delay, his self-reproaches, thus all come at crucial moments within the cat-and-mouse situation. In view of the astonishing rapidity with which Hamlet divests himself of his meditative attributes, in view of his spectacular victory which the audience could never have doubted for a moment, it becomes more difficult for us to observe a pattern of character development in the soliloquies—or anywhere else in the play.

The fifth Hamlet is the malcontent. He has no fear of meeting the Ghost since "I do not set my life at a pin's fee." This is the figure who speaks the first soliloquy:

> How weary, stale, flat, and unprofitable
> Seems to me all the uses of the world.[18]

It is he who philosophizes over the skull of poor Yorick in the presence of the clowns, standing by lest the moment become too somber. And, finally, it is this Hamlet who goes to meet his death, though it is not he who dies. We may therefore note philosophic parallels between Montaigne and *Hamlet*. But if we read the entire play in terms of such a relationship, we must ignore the four other heroes. Apparently the brooding, enlightened malcontent was an appealing figure to Shakespeare's audience. Certainly the type is prevalent enough, though the doctrine is used for the sake of disguise in Marston's *Malcontent* and adopted by Flamineo as the probable ravings of a madman in Webster's *White Devil*. In view of Shakespeare's use of feigned insanity as a dramatic device, it is perhaps not improper to regard Hamlet's grim philosophy in a related category.

If we can abstract from the play any one prevailing feature, it appears to be this: the innovation in stage art which is to be found in *Hamlet* is a dichotomy in the conception of what constitutes a dramatic situation. Man in conflict with man alternates—almost with mathematical precision—with man in conflict with himself. Shakespeare was proving that a good situation need not require two or more actors on the stage. But we must note that the internal conflict in *Hamlet,* extensional though it may be, is also an ingenious dramatic waste of time! Far from being radical or visionary, Shakespeare is probably the greatest conservative theatre craftsman the world has ever known. He was himself the ideal theatre goer. He knew what situations could be taken from his sources, even as he knew what

18 I.ii.133-34.

could be invented for maximum effectiveness. We should therefore come to see and appreciate *Hamlet* for what it is: an anthology of situations, of heroes, an index to all that could hold the Elizabethan (and subsequent) stages. It is a congeries of situations the dramatic significance of which can only be whatever happens to be going on at any given moment. Beyond this, an interpretation of *Hamlet,* as we understand the term, is not profitable or possible or necessary.

UNIVERSITY OF MIAMI

Heavenly Justice in the Tragedies
of Shakespeare

by CARMEN ROGERS

P LATO HAD SAID: Justice is wisdom, be it of man or God. In this statement of truth the world of Shakespeare concurred in principle, if
not always in deed. Its concepts of justice, civil and celestial, and
their reflection and import in Shakespearean tragedy are more easily understood when considered in relation to the general body of contemporary
thought upon matters transcendental and material. Men in Shakespeare's
plays thought much upon the universe in which they lived, upon their place
in its design, and the Power and Intelligence required to give it being. The
nature of so dynamic a power they pondered intently, with variable mood
and passion. In moments of adversity, they might, and did, feel themselves
"the first of Fortune's slaves"; might cry in bitterness:—"You partial
heavens, have I deserv'd this plague?"[1] Or, dubious of a spiritual essence
in creation, they saw only its visible physical manifestations and claimed
affinity with an intensive, self-engendered force spelled NATURE in
capitals.[2] To such a group belonged Edmund Gloucester, who, in defiance
of moral tradition regarding the bonds of humanity boasted worship of a
Nature as ruthless and amoral as himself.

> Thou, Nature, art my goddess; to thy law
> My services are bound. Wherefore should I
> Stand in plague of custom, and permit
> The curiosity of nations to deprive me.
> (*King Lear*, I.ii.1-4)

But such avowed naturalism was rare and, to most men, inadequate. It
was spiritually more reasonable and comforting to conceive of creation by
a Being capable of divine understanding and compassion, and, if need be,
discipline. Ceaselessly in the tragedies can be heard the prayers of men
desperate in the limitations of their mortality. Banquo, taunted alike by
hope and temptation, pleads:

---

1 From *Richard II*, V.v.24 and Marlowe's *The Jew of Malta*, I.ii.259.

2 Pierre de la Primaudaye, *The French Academie*, I 329 (1586). In refutation of the natural
philosophers, La Primaudaye pointed out that the very etymology of *Nature* from the
Latin *Nascor* signifies "to be borne"; hence nature "hath her creation and her birth of
God, as all other creatures haue" (p. 20).

> . . . . Merciful powers!
> Restrain in me the cursed thoughts that nature
> Gives way to in repose.
>> (*Macbeth,* II.i.7-9)

Over and over again, as though in choric chant, the distraught citizens in the tragedy of *Coriolanus* cry: "The gods preserve us!" And Coriolanus himself entreats:

> . . . . The honour'd gods
> Keep Rome in safety, and the chairs of justice
> Supplied with worthy men! plant love among us!
>> (III.iii.33-35)

The concept of heavenly justice in Shakespearean tragedy stems therefore from belief in a God (or gods,—so phrased when Shakespeare wished to set the tone of a pre-Christian era) of divine personality and immutable essence, who alone had being of himself and who, not of necessity but of free desire, created the world with "eternal and euerlasting prouidence." By laws likewise immutable, he made with right order, diversity, and rank all creatures and things, each according to his kind. God being, as Shakespeare's contemporary, Richard Hooker, wrote, "the author of nature," natural law is therefore Divine Law.[3]

To man alone of all creation was given the capacity for emulating the perfection of God:—for being, as Hamlet phrased it, noble in reason, infinite in faculty, angelic in action, godlike in apprehension.[4] With these endowments of mind and soul bestowed by the bounteous justice of Heaven, men were able to enjoy and conserve the universe in which they dwelt. Only the limitations of human will and judgment could bar them from right decision and right action. Every man must choose the extent to which he would cultivate these possessions within himself. As Plutarch had said: "Fortune is a 'counterfet Goddesse' . . . . Vice and Vertue have no masters to rule over them."[5] And as Hector commented to Paris in *Troilus and Cressida,*[6] every man "must make up a free determination 'twixt right and wrong."

Within the boundaries of a beneficent and divine order, men in the tragedies of Shakespeare are free agents. Wherever this principle is not so clarified, I believe it can be said that the magnitude and grandeur of the tragic catharsis and catastrophe are lessened. This conflict in cosmic phil-

---

3 Paragraph sources: Pierre de la Primaudaye, *The French Academie,* I, 329 (1586) and III, 658-662 (1618); John Norden *Vicissitudo Rerum* (1600) and Richard Hooker on the laws of God, nature, and man in *Of Ecclesiasticall Politie,* I.viii.3 (1593).
4 *Hamlet,* II. ii. 309-316. For one of many similar eulogies of man among the philosophers, see Pierre Boaistuau, *Theatrum Mundi,* tr. T. Alday, 1566 (?).
5 Paraphrasing in *The French Academie,* I, 468 (1586).
6 II.ii.168-171. Parallel statements in Norden's *Vicissitudo Rerum* (1600).

osophy is partially the reason that the play of *Romeo and Juliet* has more
the temper of a pathetic idyll than of an all-encompassing tragedy. Its tragic
force is also weakened by the fact that the heroes are the agencies rather
than the recipients of retribution. Through the sad fate of the lovers is
fulfilled the old Biblical promise regarding the sins of fathers.

In *Julius Caesar,* the apparent variance in philosophy is resolved long
before the play ends. Though Caesar spurns the pleas of Calphurnia with
the question,

> . . . . What can be avoided
> Whose end is purpos'd by the mighty gods?
> (II.iii.26-29)

he relies upon what he deems his own good judgment in going to the Senate.
With positiveness, Cassius comments:

> The fault, dear Brutus, is not in our stars,
> But in ourselves, that we are underlings.
> (I.ii.139-140)

The soothsayer and the oracle have foreknowledge of what will be done
by human action, but there is no suggestion ever that Cassius or Brutus
are compelled by Necessity. On the contrary, action stemming from their
own characters creates the tragic denouement.

Examples innumerable confirm the philosophy of free will in the plays
of Shakespeare. The wise Nestor observes:

> And choice, being mutual act of all our souls,
> Makes merit her election.
> (*Troilus and Cressida,* I.iii.346-349)

Scarus and Enobarbus, sickened by the ruin of the once matchless Antony,
note sardonically:

> . . . . We have kiss'd away
> Kingdoms and provinces.
> . . . . I see men's judgments are
> A parcel of their fortunes.
> (III.viii.17-18; ix.31-32)

Antony himself echoes the charge:

> I
> Have lost my way forever . . . .
> I have offended reputation,
> A most unnoble swerving . . . .
> Fortune and Antony part here.
> (III.ix.3-4,49-50; IV.x.32)

Edmund, derisive of those believing in superhuman powers, boasts sole
control of his own destiny:

> There is the excellent foppery of the world, that, when we are sick
> in fortune,—often the surfeit of our own behaviour,—we make guilty
> of our disasters the sun, the moon, and the stars; as if we were vil-
> lains by necessity, fools by heavenly compulsion, . . . treachers by
> spherical predominance . . . :and all that we are evil in, by a divine
> thrusting on: an admirable evasion of whoremaster man, to lay his
> goatish disposition to the charge of a star!
>
> (*King Lear,* I.ii.123-133)

Of Coriolanus, it was said, "This man has marr'd his fortune" (III.i.167),
when by his stubborn, proud action he alienated the citizens of Rome.

Injudiciousness is thus unsanctionable by Heaven. To operate safely
within the limits of cosmic order, human will must be girdled by other
faculties inherent in the nature of men,—intelligence and conscience. "The
law of nature," wrote La Primaudaye, "is a sence and seeing, which everie
one hath in himself, and in his conscience, whereby he discerneth betweene
good and euill."[7] The principle of heavenly justice could not in equity
exist were mankind not in possession of these endowments. The characters
in Shakespeare's plays recognize these capacities in men, even when they
ignore or ridicule them. In *Titus Andronicus,* Aaron sneers: "Thou hast a
thing within thee called conscience" (V.i.74-75); and in *The Tempest,* the
usurping and uncontrite Antonio protests: I feel not / This deity in my
bosom: twenty consciences . . . melt ere they molest!" (II.i.276-281). In
the passion of her will, Lady Macbeth seeks to disnature herself:

> Come, you spirits
> That tend on mortal thoughts!
> . . . . Make thick my blood,
> Stop up the access and passage to remorse,
> That no compunctious visitings of nature
> Shake my fell purpose . . . .
> Nor heaven peep through the blanket of the dark,
> To cry, 'Hold, hold!'

But the cool, rational mind of Claudius admits in self-judging confessional,
"O! my offense is rank, it smells to heaven"; and even Iago comes to acknowledge the presence of natural moral endowments in men, saying of
the man he hated.

> He hath a daily beauty in his life
> That makes me ugly.
>
> (*Othello,* V.i.19-20)

---

7 *The French Academie,* I, 598 (1586).

When man's violation of moral law is especially heinous, Heaven counters with comparable violence in physical phenomenon. In *King Lear,* winds crack and rage, cataracts drench the land, and Albany prays:

> If that the heavens do not their visible spirits
> Send quickly down to tame these vile offenses,
> It will come,
> Humanity must perforce prey on itself,
> Like monsters of the deep.
> 　　　(IV.ii.46-50)

In *Julius Caesar,* conspiracy begets a terrifying spectacle of warning: Men all in fire walk the streets; exhalations whiz in the air. Birds, beasts, tempests

> . . . change from their ordinance,
> Their natures, and pre-formed faculties,
> To monstrous quality.
> . . . Heaven hath infus'd them with these spirits
> To make them instruments of fear and warning
> Unto some monstrous state.
> 　　　(I.iii)

"Who ever knew the heavens menace us so?" inquires Casca. To which Cassius replies, "Those that have known the earth so full of faults."

Ironically Cassius is little aware that these dreadful heralds of heaven, these instruments of fear and warning, were sent not so much to Caesar as to himself and Brutus. The treachery to the state which they have planned in the name of patriotism is an act intolerable to celestial equity. Even the sincerity of their intent cannot excuse them.

The world of Shakespeare believed God to be the author and disposer of justice. Therefore, "justice *is* the law of God, and the bond of humane societie,"[8] With love, also emanating from God, it is implicit in natural law, whose basic tenets require loyalty to state and fraternal accord with fellow citizens, family, and friends. "Nature," observed Hector, "craves all dues be render'd to their owners."

> . . . . If this law
> Of nature be corrupted through affection, . . .
> There is a law in each well-order'd nation
> To curb those raging appetites that are
> Most disobedient and refractory.
> . . . . These moral laws
> Of nature, and of nations, speak aloud.
> . . . . To persist

---

8 *The French Academie,* I, 390-399, 411-427 (1586).

> In doing wrong extenuates not wrong,
> But makes it much more heavy.
>> (*Troilus and Cressida,* II.ii.173-188)

Civil law, at its best, is then a reflection of celestial justice through the spirit of men. The collaboration of Heaven in the dispensation of earthly justice, divinely inspired, was recognized and often sought. In the midst of the cataclysm surging without and within them, Lear, Gloucester, and even Albany petition to "ye Justicers" of heaven for aid. The Ghost of Gertrude's husband enjoins their son:

> Leave her to Heaven,
> And to those thorns that in her bosom lodge,
> To prick and sting her.
>> (*Hamlet,* I.v.86-88)

Titus, crazed with grief at the villainy about him, mutters:

> And sith there's no justice in earth nor hell,
> We will solicit heaven . . .
> To send down Justice for to wreak our wrongs.
>> (*Titus Andronicus,* IV.iii.49-51)

Said Pompey in *Antony and Cleopatra*:

> If the gods be just, they shall assist
> The deeds of justest men.
>> (II.i.1-2)

If, in ignorance, we beg for our own harms, "the wise powers deny us for our own good" (*Antony and Cleopatra,* II.i.5-7). Only cynics, such as Timon of Athens, contended: "Religious canons, civil laws are cruel" (IV. iii.60). But the good, if not always the wicked or the crazed, in Shakespearean tragedy, believe in a world guarded in justice by Heavenly power.

Yet this guardianship does not eliminate evil from the universe. Shakespeare's tragedies are set in a world where, in contempt of divine will, the wicked strive to make more furious the instruments of darkness, where the good in moments of despair see their world as a vortex of evil. For Hamlet, the time is out of joint; for Othello, Iago's villainy has dried up the fountain of happiness, turned it into a cistern, foul and deadly. Albany surveys a state in which he sees humanity preying upon itself; Lear summons the thunderbolts to "crack nature's moulds, all germens spill at once." Marcus Andronicus cries in bitterness,

> O, why should nature build so foul a den,
> Unless the gods delight in tragedies?
>> (*Titus Andronicus,* IV.i.59-60)

It is to such a background of blemished mortality that Shakespeare's concept of heavenly justice and his theory of tragedy are tied. Indissolvably, as

one structurally and philosophically, both carry his tragedies to their satisfying, though disastrous end. In them, we see vile men defy their own in-
born natures and essentially great men helpless when helplessness is fatal.
To men of faith it was sustaining to rely upon the transcendency of a divine
power to keep governance in the universe:

> In the corrupted currents of this world
> Offence's gilded hand may shove by justice,
> . . . but 'tis not so above.
> (*Hamlet,* III.iii.57-80)

It was comforting as well to believe that the discipline of a compassionate
and understanding Justice did not require absolute perfection in mortal
man. Antony was eulogized in death:

> A rarer spirit never
> Did steer humanity; but you, gods, will give us
> Some faults to make us men.
> (*Antony and Cleopatra,* V.i.31-33)

It may be said then that Shakespearean tragedy evolves from a certain
mental and spiritual incapacity in men, which may be relatively slight as in
Hamlet or, as in Macbeth, so intense that all the forces of hell seem un-
leashed. From this incapacity of the hero arises the fatal error, the *hamartia*
of Greek tragedy. This error is made sometimes deliberately, sometimes in-
advertently under adverse conditions of external pressure, but never with
foresight of the destruction it will bring. Thus tragedy could come, as
Casca flippantly suggests, from being "too saucy with the gods,"—from
the inordinate pride and insolence which, in the eyes of Heaven, seem pre-
sumptuousness to God and men; or less ignobly, it might derive from unin-
tentioned wilfulness begotten by ignorance and stunted faculties of judgment. Whatever the cause, inherently noble men violate, as Hector said,
the laws of nature and thus unintentionally set in motion their own doom.
It is as though great spiritual blindness came upon them. But sooner or
later, with the exception perhaps of Brutus, they realize their unwitting
self-destruction. The misdoer, they come to accept, must suffer.

> . . . to wilful men
> The injuries that they themselves procure
> Must be their schoolmasters.
> (*Lear,* II.iv.302-304)

Thus Justice brings the retribution that must come before moral order is
restored. Its unfolding and the hero's response to it govern the tragic plot
progression. For instance, Lear reacts with brief, impassioned defiance;
Macbeth, with persistent contempt; Hamlet, with too much self-denuncia-
tion and self-analysis. But with time, after a session of penance and remorse,

the noblest of these heroes effect a reconciliation of spirit with the celestial powers and, before life ends, attain a redemption that cleanses and elevates their souls beyond the bounds of finite being. The pity and awe felt by the spectator during the period of retribution find catharsis in watching this renewal of affinity between the hero and Heaven. Without this reconciliation, the catharsis is less complete for the spectator.

Because of restrictions in space, exemplification of these conclusions, now so generally stated, will be limited to materials in tragedies evolving from perversion of both political and private virtues. In them, Shakespeare gave particular attention to what he considered crimes against the state, —to disloyalty to the established rule and order, to men illegally seeking kingships. He agreed with La Primaudaye that "the laws of nature lead us [not only] to a monarchie"[9] but to the king ordained by Heaven. There is no hedging upon this in *Troilus and Cressida* (I.iii.78-139):

> The heavens themselves, the planets, and this centre
> Observe degree, priority, and place,
> Insisture, course, proportion, season, and form,
> Office and custom, in all line of order:
> . . . . When degree is shak'd, ...
> The enterprise is sick . . . . How could
> The primogenitive and due of birth,
> Prerogative of age, crowns, sceptres, laurels,
> But by degree, stand in authentic place?
> Take but degree away, untune that string,
> And, hark! what discord follows . . . .
> Force should be right; or rather, right and wrong—
> Between whose endless jar justice resides—
> Should lose their names, and so should justice too.

The tragedies, as well as the chronicle plays, accentuate this principle. Macbeth never forgets it, even when he foully violates it. With double irony, with dual dramatic effect, Shakespeare presents the sin of this mighty warrior who alone is trusted by the king to suppress the revolt of the traitor Macdonwald. More than finely ironic is the contrast between the ending of Macdonwald in repentence—

> . . . . Nothing in his life
> Became him like the leaving it,
> (I.iv.7-8)

and the final mood of Macbeth "supp'd full with horrors." Even in defying the rights of primogeniture, he admits the principle, when, spurred by the

---

9 *The French Academie*, I, 615 (1586).

witches' prophesies, he says hypocritically to Duncan:

> .... Our duties
> Are to your throne and state, children and servants.
>   (I.iv.24-25)

And Macduff confirms it as he exclaims, on hearing of the king's murder,—

> Confusion now hath made his masterpiece!
> Most sacrilegious murder hath broke ope
> The Lord's anointed temple, and stole thence
> The life of the building.
>   (II.iii.66-69)

In Shakespearean tragedy, treachery is unequivocally deemed one of "the villainies of nature,"—in Macbeth's own words, "against the use of nature":

> .... Stars, hide your fires!
> Let not light see my black and deep desires ....
>   (I.iv.50-52)

The deed of murder being done for ambition's sake, Shakespeare, through the symbolism of the drunken porter's ravings, makes it clear that Macbeth has become a lecher upon the sanctity of the State. Traitors, to Shakespeare as to Dante, are fit only for the last torrid circle of Hell.

The case of Justice against Brutus and Cassius is as explicit and as un-condoning, though administered with more compassion. Here it must deal with men who, in the name of patriotism, conspire against the state. With Brutus, it is undiluted devotion to state; with Cassius, it is a devotion sullied with personal envy. The flaw in Brutus is that of a man who, through public adulation and over-intent striving for Virtue, comes unhumorously to look upon himself as little less than a demi-god of goodness and right judgment. Such an attitude, in the eyes of Heaven, is nothing less than the excess of pride. Conspiracy, by whatever means it acts, by virtue or by vice, or whatever "the sufferance of souls," or "the time's abuse," is crime against both heaven and earth. With poor judgment, Brutus foresees a tyranny before it exists, considers himself and his friends "purgers, not murderers," makes kingship incompatible with benign ruling, admits of Caesar:

> I have not known when his affections sway'd
> More than his reason.
>   (II.i.20-21)

In Coriolanus, we have the more pitiable spectacle of the fatal mistake by a man once admired, but in time grossly hated. The "noble" Coriolanus, as he was eulogized even by the enemy who trampled him to death, had overlearned in youth the lesson of pride, and this arrogance assumes an extremity which the gods in heaven cannot tolerate, even in the good. The

robe of humility which he stiffly dons to win election by the mob is outward dressing really. He was, as his own mother came to recognize in sorrow, "too absolute," too utterly incapable of combining with peacetime
duties the "honour and polity" he used so well in strategies of war. But
beneath the proud, cold exterior which men saw burned the desire of a
man seeking love as well as admiration from the countrymen whom he had
served with many wounds.

When the envious tribunes turn unthinking mobs against him, wrath and
grief possess him. His "thankless country" he would see a place "of kites
and crows"; and he leaves Rome to join with Rome's enemy, saying:

> My birth-place hate I, and my love's upon
> This enemy town.
>
>   . . . .
>
> I shall be lov'd when I am lack'd . . . .
>   (*Coriolanus,* IV.iv.23-24; IV.i.15-21)

Though Coriolanus never vocally defies the gods, still this defiance is none
the less complete in his blindness to the laws of human understanding, in
his failure to continue to serve even a "canker'd country."

Thus, examples of treason or of something less than full service to one's
state continue through other Shakespearean tragedies. Antony's crime is
in yielding intemperately to personal happiness at the neglect of his country's good. The feuds of the Capulets and Montagues are, in the eyes of a
reasoning prince, the brawls of beastly men, of rebellious subjects indifferent to civil peace. In Claudius, we see the fatal disregard of divine will
regarding degree, wedlock, and creed, when he a sleeping king, his own
brother,

> Of life, of crown, of queen, at once dispatch'd . . .
> Unhousel'd, disappointed, unanel'd,
> No reckoning made . . . .
>   (*Hamlet,* I.v.75-78)

In Hamlet himself, there is a great man's failure through indecision to
restore the established order. In *King Lear,* the even more convulsive, unnatural spectacle of an old king, who should be prudent, wise, and self-
contained, but isn't. The implication is clear: even kings on thrones can
and do betray their states.

Always after such great errors in judgment and deed, the wheels of
retribution move irrevocably, quickly, impartially, but compassionately. In
so doing, Heaven works by dual means: by external agency and within the
conscience of the misdoer. The high ecstasy of Brutus and Cassius is brief.
Their hands are no sooner dipped in Caesar's blood than the forces of
Caesarism, more to be dreaded than the living Caesar, start moving to

thwart what misguided patriotism had striven to ensure. Brutus's right-eousness attains an over-smugness, takes on at times an arrogance and petty vanity. Judgment grows more ill, more fatal to the conspirators, as Cassius affectionately yields in decisions to the lesser practical judgment of Brutus. Finally, Brutus loses by insane grief the wife who has meant all to him.

Coriolanus has to sacrifice son, wife, and mother, and the only country he can ever feel his own; he has to consort in uneasy friendship and alli-ance with a rival for glory, who later does not hesitate to butt him literally into the dust. Hamlet regains too late his faculties of decision and action. Not until death does he rid his land of its "unnatural acts." And his country descends to a king who has once paid tribute to Denmark, who has fought without provocation for a plot of land "not tomb enough and con-tinent to hide the slain."

Macbeth, with his innately sensitive disposition, feels heavily the "even-handed justice," as the "Powers above put on their instruments of restitu-tion" (IV.iii). He cannot, as Caithness declares, "buckle his distemper'd cause / Within the belt of rule." The rewards and pleasures of age,

> As honour, love, obedience, troops of friends,
> I must not look to have; but, in their stead,
> Curses . . . .
>   (V.iii.15-16,24-28)

Still the scorpions in his soul newly goad him to more "Hell-broth,"—to a state of "boundless intemperance in nature" that robs him of all human virtue (IV.iii.67). Nemesis is indeed adequate when he "gins to be aweary of the sun," when life becomes to him but shadow, sound, and fury, sig-nifying nothing. The disorders of nature about him confirm "the heavens, as troubled with man's act" (II.iv.5-6). In all wise foresight, the Powers above activate the earthly agency of Macduff to restore civil order and to bring from exile the man who should be king.

The force of its discipline finished, retribution brings with varying de-gree to these men a new harmony with the universe and a new vision to replace the one-time blindness. Coriolanus regains spiritual peace in renewing fealty to his family and to his native land, though conscious that his decision will be "most mortal" to him. Brutus and Cassius gain new dignity before death, acquire a touch of heroism that they could not once claim. Brutus, perhaps never with full understanding, meets the Ghost of Caesar at Philippi and, in dying, says:

> . . . . Caesar, thou art reveng'd
> Even with the sword that kill'd thee.

To Hamlet is returned the composure and the quiet, intellectual power that had been his in former days. He has also a new confidence and a new peace. With perspective, he can now see things as they are and as they may be. Though he has "rough-hewn" his task, he knows it will be finished by the dispensation of the "divinity that shapes our ends." In this reunion of spirit with Heaven, he can say with calmness:

> Since no man has aught of what he leaves, what is't
> to leave betimes?

In *King Lear,* against a background of defiance, inhumanity, and division in government unparalleled in any other tragedy, celestial justice dispenses its discipline with the greatest magnitude and with greatest terror to the spectator. "Unwhipp'd of justice" on earth, men's passions despoil the universe. The fury of Lear's striving

> . . . . in his little world of man to out-scorn
> The to-and-fro-conflicting wind and rain
> (III.i.4-15)

is a vivid symbol of impenitent men contesting the power of Heaven.

In Lear's personal tragedy, Shakespeare depicts with slow, measured detail the awe and yet the grandeur of a soul battling for the cleansing that must come to it before it can have peace. The evil of his wrath and of his little wisdom is purged in the blasts of the storm that, like Justice, makes no distinctions between king and beggar: "Here's a night," said the Fool, "pities neither wise men nor fool."

In the community of sorrow in the hovel, Lear comes to know human compassion:

> You houseless poverty, ...
> Poor naked wretches, wheresoe'er you are . . .
> Take physic, pomp . . . .
> And show the heavens more just.
> (III.iv.24-36)

Finally, by the physic of his purging, passion is wasted and "oppress'd nature sleeps." Retribution, rebellion, remorse, reconciliation, and eventually redemption are all in the play. Love and justice restore sanity both to Lear and the State. In humility, Lear can say to Cordelia,—"I am a very foolish fond old man." Kingdoms, knights, and protestations of love now lack consequence. The gods, he knows, are just, and he is wiser:

> . . . . Come, let's away to prison . . .
> And take upon's the mystery of things,
> As if we were God's spies.
> (V.ii.8-19)

In each of the great tragedies, the redemption is clear, though less moving than in *Lear;* and the catharsis is full and satisfying both to hero and spectator, except with Macbeth, who never attains redemption nor regains the respect of the world he once defied. He alone remains in the hearts of his countrymen the "monster" he had become. To them, his is "the usurper's cursed head." Though the compassion of Heaven is great and it showers Macbeth with pity, it could not give him in death the benediction that was bestowed upon other Shakespearean heroes. Men, cognizant alike of both earthly and heavenly justice, petition the angels to sing Hamlet to rest. Young Antony, in generous but fair judgment, is prompted to say of Brutus: He did all only "in general honest thought and common good to all." Of Lear, Kent murmured:

> . . . he hates him
> That would upon the rack of this tough world
> Stretch him out longer.

"The gods are just," mused Edgar. And the newly chastened Edmund adds:

> Thou hast spoken right, 'tis true;
> The wheel is come full circle; I am here.

And Lear, with a perception begotten alike of celestial discipline and celestial mercy, comforts his daughter as they are taken to execution:

> Upon such sacrifices, my Cordelia,
> The gods themselves throw incense.

FLORIDA STATE UNIVERSITY

Shylock and the Puritan Usurers

by PAUL N. SIEGEL

O
F WHAT," writes E. E. Stoll (*From Shakespeare to Joyce*, New York, 1944, p. 134), "would the figure of Shylock remind the audience? Of Jews at first hand they may have known little. There were Jews in England, but illegally and by connivance . . . He would rather remind them of the precisians and Pharisees in their midst, who 'put on gravity,' were keen on money and, more than other Christians, addicted to usury. They, too, were given to biblical phrasing and scriptural allusions, preferably of the Old Dispensation. They Hebraized, in short. Shylock would not be taken for a Puritan with a capital letter, and was not meant to be. Yet the Elizabethans could hardly help thinking of the Rabbi Zeal-of-the-Lands, the Ananiases and Tribulations round about them, if not as yet upon the stage; and it is not unlikely that such picturesque customers as these offered suggestions to Shakespeare's imagination."

Stoll's remarks are in keeping with recent scholarship such as that of Lily B. Campbell and John W. Draper which has shown Shakespeare's plays as bringing to his audience a world that, although remote in time or place, was reminiscent of contemporary England. His belief that Shylock would have reminded Shakespeare's audience of the Puritans of its own day gives us in the romantic world built from familiar folk material of *The Merchant of Venice*, with its lovely lady sought, like the golden fleece, by suitors from all over the world, its fairy-tale set of conditions by which she is to be won, its diabolical heartless Jew of medieval legend, one in which the audience could catch piquant resemblances to the world with which it was familiar. The connection between the villainous Jewish money-lender of folk tradition whom Shakespeare made a richly colorful figure, the member of an alien, exotic race, and the Elizabethan Puritan usurer is not pointed up by any allusion in the play. However, a contemporary audience, alive to the issues of its own time, does not need the pointers that posterity does. Maxwell Anderson, who has learned from the Shakespearean practice of universalizing the contemporary through the historical and making the historical immediate through the contemporary, recently presented in his *Barefoot in Athens* a historical play which the reviewers immediately recognized as implying, as one of them put it, "a reasonable parallel between the pressures which were once brought to bear on Socrates and those which are intimidating free men today." It is such a generally current concern which

Stoll's belief implies. I propose to give evidence for his belief by citing
expressions of Elizabethan opinion which serve to show that Judaism,
Puritanism and usury were connected in the popular mind and that many
of Shylock's traits would have reminded Shakespeare's audience of the
Puritan usurers of its own time.

Usury, as R. H. Tawney has shown, was a burning social problem in
Elizabethan times.[1] Always excoriated, the money-lender now played a
more important role than ever in the economic life of the country, squeez-
ing landowners, many of whom were impoverished by having to depend
on fixed rents at a time of rising prices, and craftsmen, who were no
longer producing for a local market but were part of a complex commercial organization and needed credit to maintain production. He was seen
as an arrant individualist disrupting for his own selfish purposes the traditional relationships of the hierarchical society demanded by the laws of
man's nature. "That ouglie, detestable and hurtefull synne of usurie," wrote
Thomas Wilson,

> caries many a mischief linked into it in nature, the same synne beinge
> nowe so ranke throughout all Englande, not in London onelye, that
> men have altogether forgotten free lending, and have geven themselves
> wholye to lyve by fowle gayning, makinge the lone of monye a kinde of
> merchandise, a thing directlye against all lawe, against nature, and
> against god. And what should this meane, that, in steade of charitable
> dealing, and the use of almose (for lending is a spice thereof), hardnes
> of harte hath nowe gotten place, and greedie gayne is cheefelye folowed,
> and horrible extorcion commonly used? I do verely believe, the ende of
> thys worlde is nyghe at hande.[2]

In Shylock is embodied this "ouglie, detestable and hurtefull synne of
usurie."[3] Greedy and hardhearted, without mercy or charity, sophistically
defending usury as a legitimate business practice, "a kinde of merchandise,"
he is contrasted with Antonio, the "royal merchant"[4] of Venice, a Christian
gentleman who is a figure of romance, gracious, generous, and charitable,
lending freely without interest, ready to sacrifice his life for his friend in
accordance with the ideal the Renaissance gentleman inherited from chivalry.

But the contemporary usurer, Wilson repeats several times, is worse
than the medieval Jewish money-lender, for the Jewish money-lender was

1 Cf. R. H. Tawney's editorial introduction, Thomas Wilson, *A Discourse Upon Usury*
[1572] (New York, 1925).
2 Wilson, p. 177.
3 John W. Draper, "Usury in *The Merchant of Venice*," Modern Philology, XXXIII
(1935), 37-47, showed the importance of the contemporary economic situation and of
contemporary attitudes toward usury for an understanding of Shylock. He made, however, no mention of Puritanism.
4 IV, i, 29.

at least following his own laws and not pretending to be a member of the Christian commonwealth. And the typical contemporary usurer is the Puritan. "[The 'dissembling gospeller'] under the colour of religion over-throweth all religion, and bearing good men in hande that he loveth play-nesse, useth covertlie all deceypte that may bee, and for pryvate gayne undoeth the common welfare of man. And touching thys sinne of usurie, none doe more openly offende in thys behalfe than do these counterfeite professours of thys pure religion."[5] So too Marston describes a "seeming saint" who "with his bait of usury/ He bit me in deepest usury./ No Jew, no Turk, would use a Christian/ So inhumanely as this Puritan."[6]

Indeed the Puritans, because of their emphasis on Old Testament law, had from the start of the religious controversy been charged with returning to Judaism. Bishop Whitgift, arguing with Thomas Cartwright, told him that he did "Judaizare, 'play the Jew.' "[7] It was a charge that continued to be frequently made, as we can infer from Zeal-of-the-land Busy's excuse for attending the fair (Jonson's work was written after *The Merchant of Venice,* but the quotation, like other such quotations I shall use, seems to imply a long-standing attitude): "There may be a good vse made of it, too, now I think on't: by the publike eating of Swines flesh, to profess our hate, and loathing of Iudaisme, whereof the brethren stand taxed."[8] The extreme Puritan sects such as the Family of Love, which was being at-tacked as early as the 1590's, seem indeed, in their adherence to Old Testament law, to have adopted religious observances usually regarded as peculiarly Jewish. "I am a Puritan," says one of the characters in Daven-port's *New Trick to Cheat the Devil* (IV.i),

> One that will eat no pork,
Doth use to shut his shop on Saturdays,
And open them on Sundays; a Familist
And one of the arch limbs of Belzebub
A Jewish Christian and a Christian Jew.

From their close and continued reading of the Old Testament, Puritans became saturated with its diction. Many, as we can see from Middleton's *The Family of Love* and Jonson's *The Alchemist,* assumed Hebrew names[9] and zealously studied Hebrew.[10] Like the Old Testament Jews, they thought

---

5 Wilson, p. 178.
6 John Marston, *Works,* ed. A. H. Bullen (London, 1887), III, 271. Cf. Robert Greene's picture of Gorinius, the Machiavellian usurer (*The Life and Complete Works,* ed. Alexander B. Grosart, London, 1881-3, XII, 104): "He was religious too, neuer without a booke at his belt, and a bolt in his mouth, ready to shoote through his sinfull neighbor." See R. H. Tawney, *Religion and the Rise of Capitalism* (New York, 1926), pp. 232-3, for later identifications of usury and Puritanism.
7 *The Works of John Whitgift, D. D.,* ed. John Ayre (Parker Society, 1851), I, 271.
8 *Bartholomew Fair,* I, vi, 93-6.
9 Cf. Middleton, *The Family of Love,* III, iii, 59.
10 Cf. *The Alchemist,* II, v, 334.

of themselves as a chosen people, looking upon the Anglican Church as idolatrous. They in turn were regarded as a minority of foreigners, having imported their religion from Geneva and adopted a strange attire and strange manners, such as talking through their nose. These similarities between the Puritans and the Jews must have given point to the identification of Puritanism and Judaism. They made it possible for Shakespeare to suggest that Jewish moneylenders and Puritan usurers were kindred spirits in their villainy and in their comically outlandish grotesqueness.

The common accusation made by the satirists and dramatists against the Puritans was that they were hypocrites. Thus Nashe includes under hypocrisy "all Machiavilisme, puritanisme, and outward gloasing with a mans enemie."[11] Critics who have sought to soften Shakespeare's picture of Shylock have failed to notice his consummate hypocrisy, accepting his statement that his proposal of a pound of flesh as surety is a "merry sport"[12] and finding that he only desires payment after his thirst for revenge has been aroused by the elopement of Jessica. But Shylock is not a man for "merry sport." As soon as Antonio enters, Shylock expresses in soliloquy his profound hatred for him as a Christian who brings down the rate of interest by lending gratis in "low simplicity" (the audience would have understood it to be in Christian charity), concluding (I.iii.42-53), "Cursèd be my tribe,/ If I forgive him." When Bassanio interrupts his evil meditations with "Shylock, do you hear?" he pretends to have been mentally casting up his accounts to see if he can make up the sum required by Bassanio. To Antonio he addresses himself courteously: "Rest you fair, good signior;/ Your worship was the last man in our mouths." Antonio had indeed been spoken of just before he entered, but not in the affable manner which Shylock implies. Shylock in fact was, as Antonio had appeared, rejecting with fierce contempt for the eaters of pork an invitation to dine with him. Now, when Antonio impatiently asks if he will grant the loan, as he is characteristically delaying his answer in Levantine bargaining fashion, Shylock reveals in a flash of indignation his rancor, inquiring with bitter irony if, in return for Antonio's insults, he should "bend low and in a bondsman's key" offer to lend him money now that Antonio needs his financial aid. When Antonio, however, does not act the suppliant but forthrightly says that he will insult him again, telling him that if he wishes to lend him the money, he should do so as an enemy, for friendship would not permit the taking of interest, he changes his tone, cringing obsequiously:

Why, look you, how you storm!

---

11 *The Works of Thomas Nashe*, ed R. B. McKerrow (London, 1904), I, 220. See also, for instance, Wilson, Marston, and Greene, quoted above.
12 I, iii, 146.

> I would be friends with you and have your love,
> Forget the shames that you have stain'd me with,
> Supply your present wants and take no doit
> Of usance for my moneys, and you'll not hear me:
> This is kind I offer.

This is indeed spoken "in a bondsman's key." Shylock acts like the cur he has been called by Antonio, snapping viciously when he thinks he can do so with impunity but immediately returning to bootlicking when he is met with a show of strength. His refusal to make an open and above-board deal as an avowed enemy, as Antonio proposes, his profession of friendship after his momentary revelation of the hatred concealed beneath his "patient shrug," his offer to lend without interest after his defense of usury stamp him as a hypocrite of the worst sort. The audience, which has already heard Shylock tell what he will do if he catches Antonio "once upon the hip,"[13] is not permitted to be in doubt about his intention in proposing the bond. "I like not fair terms and a villain's mind," warns Bassanio, concluding a couplet at the close of the scene, but he is over-ridden by the devoted Antonio, who does not fear to incur any dangers which would enable him to help his friend.

Until Shylock announces his desire for revenge in a burst of rage, he continues hypocritical. In spite of his previously declared religious scruples at dining with Christians, he accepts Bassanio's invitation to join him in the fellowship of the banquet-table, but he goes "in hate, to feed upon/ The prodigal Christian."[14] So too does he recommend Launcelot Gobbo to Bassanio, not out of friendliness to either, but with the design of ridding himself of a heavy-eating, inefficient servant and fastening him as an added expense upon Bassanio.

Puritan hypocrisy was generally portrayed as taking the form of a pretence of being better than other men, and the Puritan was presented as stiff-necked rather than obsequious, but he could be made on occasion to be self-abasing if it served his need. Thus Tribulation in *The Alchemist* submits to humiliating conditions involving denials of his religious principles in order that Subtle might counterfeit money for him, just as Shylock goes to dine at Bassanio's in order to help ruin him. Shylock, on the other hand, can be as self-righteous as any Puritan. "O father Abram," he exclaims, "what these Christians are,/ Whose own hard dealings teaches them suspect/ The thoughts of others!"[15] He thinks of himself as belonging to a "sacred nation"[16] and affirms "sufferance is the badge of all our

---

13 I. iii, 47.
14 II, v, 14-5.
15 I, iii, 161-3.
16 I, iii, 49.

tribe,"[17] just as Tribulation says, "These chastisements are common to the *Saints,*/ And such rebukes we of the *Separation*/ Must beare with willing shoulder, as the trialls,/ Sent forth, to tempt our frailties."[18]

Shylock's pharisaism, like that of the Puritans, takes the form of conempt for merry-making and revelry. "What, are there masques?" he exclaims in the very accents of the Puritan;

> Hear you me, Jessica:
> Lock up my doors; and when you hear the drum
> And the vile squealing of the wry-neck'd fife,
> Clamber not you up to the casements then,
> Nor thrust your head into the public street
> To gaze on Christian fools with varnish'd faces,
> But stop my house's ears, I mean my casements:
> Let not the sound of shallow foppery enter
> My sober house.[19]

His grim austerity and niggardliness of spirit are contrasted with the liberality of Bassanio. Launcelot, famished in Shylock's service, applies to become the servant of Bassanio, who gives rare new liveries, and has his suit immediately granted. Launcelot acts as the same sort of touchstone as Feste in *Twelfth Night*. Malvolio, described by Maria in her character-sketch of him as "a kind of puritan"[20] who, however, as Puritans were so often charged with being, really cares about his own material advancement rather than his religion, calls Feste "a barren rascal."[21] He is rebuked by the Countess Olivia, who tells him that those who are "generous, guiltless and of free disposition"[22] graciously permit liberties in a fool which the humorless Malvolio would deny. So too does Shylock fail to understand the humor of the clown who, as Jessica says, robbed his house "of some taste of tediousness."[23] His narrow, ungenerous mind, meanly re-

---

17 I, iii, 111.
18 *The Alchemist*, III, i, 1-4.
19 II, v, 28-36. Shylock's despising of the music of the fife and drum reveals his harsh, inharmonious nature. Antonio's calm serenity in preparing to sacrifice his life for his friend contrasts with his raging hatred, which blinds him to every consideration of pity, mercy, and even self-interest, making him refuse three times the sum due him rather than give up his pound of flesh. "I do oppose/ My patience to his fury," Antonio says (IV, i, 10-3), "and am arm'd/ To suffer, with a quietness of spirit,/ The very tyranny and rage of his." Lorenzo's words in the fifth act (V, i, 83-88), in which harmony is restored to Belmont after the disquieting disturbance of the news of Antonio's trial, apply to Shylock:
> The man that hath no music in himself,
> Nor is not moved with concord of sweet sounds,
> Is fit for treasons, stratagems and spoils;
> The motions of his spirit are dull as night
> And his affections dark as Erebus:
> Let no such man be trusted.
20 II, iii, 151.
21 I, v, 90.
22 I, v, 99.
23 II, iii, 3.

stricted to money-making, renders him incapable of unbending to laughter; it is the antithesis of the well-rounded personality of the Renaissance gentleman Bassanio.

Like the morally rigid Puritans, Shylock is intolerant of others and attributes to them his own spiritual defects. Immediately after Launcelot has pointed up for us the contrast between Bassanio's munificence and his miserliness, he tells Launcelot that Bassanio will not allow him to eat and sleep all day long as he did. When the princely merchant Antonio enters, he comments to himself, "How like a fawning publican he looks,"[24] unwittingly echoing the Pharisee's words about the Publican in the parable.[25] And, after having said with hypocritical humility that "sufferance," patient endurance, is the badge of all his tribe, he justifies his lust for revenge by saying that he has learned it from the Christians. "If a Christian wrong a Jew, what should his sufferance be by Christian example? Why, revenge."[26] But the event is to show the difference between Christian mercy and the ferocious vengefulness which he has hidden under his "sufferance."

Shylock's malevolence is presented as diabolically inhuman. Medieval literature had given the story of man's redemption in the symbolic form of his being freed by the "ransom" of Christ from a bond to the Devil, an unrelenting creditor with the characteristics of a usurer.[27] The Jew had also been portrayed as a devil serving Satan.[28] Shakespeare continued the tradition, having Shylock referred to as a devil again and again.[29] But Puritans as well as Jews were called devils in Shakespeare's time. Anglicans, who, being sure that they were on the side of the angels, regarded all those not of their party as being of the devil's party, made "the Devil is a Puritan" a cant phrase.[30] The pious exterior of the Puritan, it was charged, concealed the spirit of the Devil. Those who owed money to a Puritan usurer found that they had the devil to pay. "Do you call us devils?" exclaims a creditor in Middleton's *A Trick to Catch the Old One* (IV.iv.322). "You shall find us puritans—Bear him away; let 'em talk as they go." The Devil in the guise of a Puritan was more relentlessly cruel than ever.

With the Bibliolotry of the Puritans it was inevitable that the saying

24 I, iii, 42.
25 Luke, xviii, 10-14.
26 III, i, 73-5.
27 Benjamin N. Nelson, *The Idea of Usury, From Tribal Brotherhood to Universal Other-hood* (Princeton University Press, 1949), p. 144n.
28 E. E. Stoll, *Shakespeare Studies* (New York, 1927), pp. 270-1. Stoll's study is, of course, fundamental for an understanding of "the Jew that Shakespeare drew."
29 I, iii, 99; II, ii, 23-6; II, iii, 2; III, i, 22-24; III, ii, 35; IV, i, 217.
30 William P. Holden, "The Religious Controversy and Anti-Puritan Satire, 1572-1642," unpublished Harvard doctoral thesis, p. 266. I am grateful to Dr. Holden for lending me his personal copy of his thesis and for his scholarly courtesy in volunteering information.

about the Devil citing scripture be applied to them. In *A Merry Knack to Know a Knave* (1592), when a beggar asks a Puritan preacher for alms, the preacher twists Scripture to justify a refusal: "And in good time, look in the blessed Proverb of Solomon, which is Good deeds do not justify a man; therefore, I count it sin to give thee anything."[31] "The answer," observes Holden, "is a piece of theological web-spinning typical of the stage Puritan when he would get himself out of moral difficulties."[32] Thus too does Shylock cite Jacob's acumen in his business gamble with his brother to justify the taking of interest, a citation whose fallacy is exposed when, in reply to Antonio's pointed question, "Did he take interest," Shylock has to hem and haw (I.iii.76-8): "No, not take interest, not, as you would say,/ Directly interest."[33] Antonio's comment on Shylock's sophistry is like Honesty's comment on the sophistry of the Puritan preacher in *A Merry Knack to Know a Knave*: "See how he can turn and wind scripture to his own use." "Mark you this, Bassanio," says Antonio (I.iii.98-103),

> The devil can cite Scripture for his purpose.
> An evil soul producing holy witness
> Is like a villain with a smiling cheek,
> A goodly apple rotten at the heart:
> O, what a goodly outside falsehood hath![34]

In the trial scene "this cruel devil," as Bassanio calls him (IV.i.217),

---

31 Dodsley, *Old Plays*, VI (1875), 580. Quoted by Holden, p. 265.
32 Holden, p. 265.
33 Shylock's talmudical manner of citing Scripture, with its repetitions and involutions and its show of learning, is similar to Puritan biblical exegesis. Compare Shylock's turn of speech with Zeal-of-the-land Busy's.
  Shylock. When Jacob grazed his uncle Laban's sheep—
  This Jacob from our holy Abram was,
  As his wise mother wrought in his behalf,
  The third possessor; ay, he was the third— I, iii, 72-5.
  Busy. Verily, for the disease of longing, it is a disease, a carnall disease, or appetite, incident to women: and as it is carnall, and incident, it is naturall, very naturall: Now Pigge, it is a meat, and a meat that is nourishing, and may be long'd for, and so consequently eaten: but in the Fayre, and as a *Bartholomew*-pig, it cannot be eaten, for the very calling it a *Bartholomew*-pigge, and to eat it so, is a spice of *Idolatry.*"— I, vi, 48-55.
34 The difference between counterfeit appearance and reality is central to *The Merchant of Venice*, both in the story of the "merry bond" (I, iii, 174) which Shylock offers in his false friendship and in the story of the three caskets, in the least auspicious-looking of which lies Portia's portrait, the beautiful representation of the fair prize of Portia herself. Bassanio is able to win Portia because he sees beyond her material riches and physical beauty to her spiritual riches and beauty. She is, he tells Antonio (I, i, 161-3), not only "richly left" and "fair," but, "fairer than that word,/ Of wondrous virtues." When, at the crucial moment in the love story, he has to choose between the three caskets and, inspired by the song about "fancy," short-lived physical fascination, meditates on the theme "So may the outward shows be least themselves," he illustrates it by the hypocritically pious use of Scripture for foul purposes deemed characteristic of the Puritans (III, ii, 77-80):
          In religion,
  What damned error, but some sober brow
  Will bless it and approve it with a text,
  Hiding the grossness with fair ornament?
The illustration serves to link the two plots thematically.

who has cited Scripture and whose language is full of Old Testament allusions and phraseology, insists on his pound of flesh, holding to the strict letter of the law. The Puritans had demanded undeviating adherence to the Mosaic code, whose severe penalties included death for blasphemy and adultery. Whitgift, contending that the teachings of the New Testament had superseded the Mosaic code, had pointed out that the Puritan demand meant that a small body of laws would be rigorously enforced without regard to the modifications, exceptions, and nullifications of it that had grown up through national legislation and judicial precedent and that "the prince must be abridged of that prerogative which she hath in pardoning such as by the law be condemned to die."[35] Shylock, in his stubborn insistence (IV.i.42), "I stand here for law," is dramatizing the doctrinal inflexibility of the Puritans, which, it was charged, would deprive the prince of his power to exercise that which, as Portia says (IV.i.189), becomes him "better than his crown"—his mercy.

For his insistence that the engine of the law be used on his victim in all its rigors Shylock suffers dramatic retribution. Three times does Portia give him the opportunity to save himself by being merciful, and three times does Shylock refuse it. Christian charity, freely given, he cannot understand—"I cannot find it; 'tis not in the bond."[36] "My deeds upon my head! I crave the law," he exclaims in answer to Portia's statement that the Lord's Prayer "doth teach us all to render/ The deeds of mercy."[37] Having chosen the law rather than mercy, he finds that the law swings back upon him, like a crank too tightly wound reversing itself to spin in the face of the person winding it. "Is that the law?"[38] he exclaims in stupefied amazement when Portia delivers her sudden stroke. "Thyself shalt see the act," replies Portia, "For, as thou urgest justice, be assured/ Thou shalt have justice, more than thou desirest." The warning of the Sermon on the Mount, echoed by the Duke,[39] comes true: "Be ye therefore merciful, as your Father also is merciful. Judge not, and ye shall not be judged: condemn not, and ye shall not be condemned: forgive, and ye shall be forgiven . . . For with what measure ye mete, with the same shall men mete to you again."[40]

Shakespeare, in the resolution of the trial scene, had to make the audience feel that dramatic justice had been dispensed and yet that Christ-

---

35 Whitgift, I, 273. Behind the religious dispute lay the question of political power, towards which the Puritan bourgeoisie was groping. Whitgift saw (III, 273) the Puritans as seeking a theocracy in which the presbyters would be supreme.
36 IV, i, 262.
37 IV, i, 314.
38 IV, i. 314.
39 "How shalt thou hope for mercy rendering none?"—IV, i, 88.
40 Luke, vi, 36-8. The same text furnishes the basis and the title for *Measure for Measure*, which has many parallels with *The Merchant of Venice*. *Measure for Measure* is concerned with the exposure of the puritanical Angelo who in his self-righteousness has no sympathy for human frailties and wishes to enforce the law in all its severity. "Lord

ian mercy, contrasting with the conduct of Shylock, had been shown; he had to rouse it to derisive laughter at the sight of the biter, "the dog Jew,"[41] being bit, and yet he had to kindle a glow of moral superiority. He did so by having Shylock ignominiously retrace his steps, first expressing readiness to accept thrice the principal that he had spurned, next expressing readiness to accept the principal itself, then seeking only to get away without further ado—and finally, when he is brought grovelling, to the jeers of Gratiano mockingly repeating Shylock's exultant exclamations concerning Portia's justice, receiving mercy. It is a mercy that is freely and generously given. The Duke's prerogative, prescribed by law, is to spare the culprit's life. Not only does he do so before Shylock can ask for it; he mitigates the law, promising that the state will accept a fine instead of half of Shylock's wealth. When the miserly Shylock exclaims that losing his money and losing his life are the same to him, Antonio has his opportunity to be merciful. He asks the Duke to remit the fine and foregoes his half of Shylock's money, stipulating that it be held in trust by him to go to Lorenzo and Jessica after Shylock's death and that Shylock become a Christian. Thus Shylock has granted to him his life, half of his wealth and, so an Elizabethan audience would have believed, the possibility of achieving salvation. Yet in his enforced provision for his daughter and in his reduction from scornful obduracy to abject humility dramatic justice is satisfied.

At the end of the play Portia acts as a kind of a presiding deity bestowing rewards upon all from her limitless riches. She informs Antonio, who has followed the injunction (Luke.vi.38), "Give, and it shall be given unto you," that the waters have brought back his argosies, laden with treasure. She announces to Lorenzo his inheritance of Shylock's wealth. And she pardons Bassanio, who has kept the spirit if not the letter of her commandment in giving away her ring, giving him herself in the happy consummation of their marriage. Thus do aristocratic largess, identified with Christian charity, and chivalric friendship and chivalric love triumph over the Puritan individualism that, in cracking through the shell of the old order, was substituting what Thomas Carlyle was to call the "cash nexus" for the older idealized relationships.

RIPON COLLEGE

Angelo is precise," says the Duke, telling of his plan to test him (I, iii, 50-4),
    Stands at a guard with envy; scarce confesses
    That his olood flows, or that his appetite
    Is more to bread than stone: hence shall we see,
    If power change purpose, what our seemers be.
"Precise" is, of course, the Elizabethan vernacular adjectival form of "precisian," Puritan. For a study of *Measure for Measure* as reflecting the religious controversy, see Donald J. McGinn, "The Precise Angelo," *Joseph Quincy Adams Memorial Studies*, ed. James G. McManaway *et al.* (Washington, D. C., 1948), pp. 129-39.
41 II, viii, 14.

The Problem of Ophelia

By J. MAX PATRICK

TRADITIONALLY Shakespeare's Ophelia has been interpreted in two different ways. Usually she is thought to be an innocent girl, who caught up in tragic events, loses her mind and drowns. This familiar *sentimental estimate* is supported by a considerable body of evidence, probability, tradition, and dramatic effectiveness and needs no elaboration here. Less well known is the view that Ophelia was Hamlet's mistress, an interpretation which is sometimes extended to the possibility that she became pregnant and that pregnancy was a cause of her suicide. Because this *erotic estimate* is less widely known, there is need to elaborate upon it.

The erotic estimate is rooted in the ancient Hamlet legend. In the various forms and literary treatments of this legend before Shakespeare, Ophelia or her prototype was usually a loose woman. For example, in the *Hystorie of Hamblet,* the King's advisers sought to trap the Prince by setting "some faire and beawtifull woman in a secret place . . . to allure his mind to have pleasure of her." For reasons stated later, it may be conjectured that Ophelia was a comic, erotic role in the *Hamlet,* probably by Thomas Kyd, which is believed to have preceded Shakespeare's versions.

In Shakespeare's play (the Kittredge text), Ophelia is persistently associated with the *idea* of unchastity and, to a lesser extent, with the idea of innocence. Almost as soon as she is introduced, Laertes warns her not to open her chaste treasure to Hamlet's importunity, and Polonius repeats the warning lest she tender him a fool. She next appears to tell how Hamlet had forced himself into her private room. A little later, Polonius decides to "loose" her to Hamlet. As Dover Wilson has pointed out, cows are loosed to bulls for breeding, and Polonius's agricultural use of the term is indicated by his resolve to keep a farm if he is wrong. Ophelia is again associated with the idea of unchastity when Hamlet tells Polonius how the sun breeds maggots and demands, "Have you a daughter?" The Prince's next speech is explicit: "Conception is a blessing, but not as your daughter may conceive." In the scene where Ophelia is "loosed," her chastity is no longer taken for granted. Almost immediately he cries, "Are you honest?" and talks of honesty (chastity) being transformed into a bawd. He even urges her to enter a nunnery lest she breed sinners. By *nunnery* Shakespeare may have intended *bawdy-house,* a popular usage among the anti-papal

Elizabethans. Although the idea of innocence is reintroduced, Hamlet condemns it as false, telling Ophelia that though she be chaste as snow, she shall not escape calumny, for women make wantonness their ignorance. The unchastity motif is struck again when she is introduced in the play scene. Hamlet asks if he shall lie in her lap, puns on country matters, stresses the sexual meaning of *lying,* and even transforms Ophelia's "I think nothing," into sexual symbolism. When their conversation is renewed, he intrudes sexual significance into her comment that he is keen: it would take a groaning to take off his edge.

When Ophelia goes mad, she makes the association with unchastity herself. Indeed, her songs may have a chorus function in the play and provide a key to its interpretation, as do songs and utterances of fools and madmen in other Shakespearean plays.

In Act IV, scene 5, Ophelia is troubled by two things: the death of her father and "tricks i' the' world," that is, a lover who, having seduced a maiden, leaves her to her fate. Both elements are detectable in the song about the lover dead and gone. Certainly Hamlet is in effect "dead and gone," though not as her father was dead. When the King claims that the conceit is upon Ophelia's father, she corrects him. Discarding his interpretation, she explains "what it means" by the Valentine ballad. It tells how a maid came to a man's window. Rising from his bed, he dons his clothes, an action which seems to indicate that he has no designs upon her. But she insists on entrance and so loses her virginity. Somewhat unconvincingly under the circumstances, the third stanza projects the blame on the youth: "Young men will do't, if they come to't./By cock, they are to blame." The nature of the guilt is explained in the last stanza: previous to the misdeed, the youth had promised to marry the girl. However, he has a defence: "So would I ha' done, by yonder sun,/If thou hadst not come to my bed."

Does this song summarize a relationship between Hamlet and Ophelia? It *suggests* such a relationship, and it coheres with much of the rest of the play: the warnings against Hamlet given by Laertes and Polonius, Hamlet's oppressive sense of his own guilt, and the tendency which a guilty man would have to delay punishing a fellow sinner. It helps to explain why Hamlet was so insulting to Ophelia in the play scene and why he condemned women for painting and wantonness. If the song is to be taken seriously, it would suggest that Ophelia had been secretly bethrothed to Hamlet, or at least that she had visited and given herself to him. The final lines may imply that after intimacy, Hamlet refused to marry her—a confirmation of his dictum that there would be no more marriages. In any case, a song on such a theme is enough to suggest to an audience that Ophelia may have been pregnant and that her condition and Hamlet's refusal to marry caused the suicide. The objections raised by the priest in connection with her funeral point to the same interpretation. He remarks that because her death was doubtful, shards, flints, and pebbles should have been thrown on her. Such was the usual penalty for suicide. But he would have added a further ignominy and would have treated the corpse as if the girl were an adultress: he would have denied her virgin crants and maiden strewments. Again Ophelia and the idea of unchastity are associated.

Evidence in the play is insufficient to prove either Ophelia's innocence or guilt. Shakespeare repeatedly associated her with the idea of unchastity but left his audience uncertain as to her guilt, probably inclined to believe that she was chaste. The judgment of an audience would depend largely on the acting and production of a particular performance. However, it would seem that Shakespeare intended Ophelia to be acted in such a way that the *possibility* of her unchastity would occur to any intelligent, unprejudiced spectator. The possibility is likely to be rejected, but its consideration is dramatically significant.

How audiences in Shakespeare's day reacted to Ophelia is not known with any certainty. However, it is a commonplace that Elizabethan audiences tended to find madness fascinatingly amusing. In *The Changeling* by Middleton and Rowley, watching lunatics is called "a pitiful delight," "a mirth in madness" (III.iii.31,33), and a "frightful pleasure" (III.iv. 284), and arrangements are made to round off the revels at a marriage by displaying madmen! Is it not probable that at least part of Shakespeare's audience found the bawdiness of Ophelia's songs amusing and that they laughed at her garlands of weeds, her dispensing of worthless herbs, and other manifestations of her insanity? If they did so, that fact is no proof that Shakespeare intended such a reaction: the pathos of the insanity is apparent to any sensitive reader of the play. Nevertheless, Shakespeare, familiar with the theater and its audience, must have been aware that a ribald reaction was possible.

Such a reaction was to be expected. Shakespeare's play was a revision of an earlier *Hamlet* attributed to Kyd. Though lost, this play may be characterized with some confidence as a drama in which revenge was a dominating passion: it was a tragedy of blood, sensationalism, and ranting. Ophelia in it was probably a crude, somewhat erotic character. Kyd based his play on Belleforest's *Histoires Tragiques,* in which, as Charlton M. Lewis notes, there was already "a vague suggestion of the story of Ophelia and a curious hint of the comic aspect of insanity."[1]

1 Charlton M. Lewis, *The Genesis of Hamlet* (New York, 1907), p. 41.

Another observation by Lewis, that Ophelia's part is put together care-lessly in Shakespeare's final version of *Hamlet*,[2] seems to indicate that Shakespeare retained some materials from the Kydian version and failed to harmonize them completely, or, more probably, that he retained enough of the older version to enable those who had seen it to interpret the revised play in the traditional fashion as a tragedy of blood and revenge whose heroine is both crude and comic in her madness. Other seventeenth-century plays on similar themes depict the heroine as the hero's mistress. In Chet-tle's *Hoffman. or a Revenge for a Father* (1602), Lucibella, the equivalent of Ophelia, loses both husband and father and goes mad. She sings "Downe, downe a downe, hey downe," and adds that she sang it "while Luodwick slept with me." Ophelia may have acted likewise. Moreover, in Suckling's *Aglaura* (1637), which is obviously modeled upon *Hamlet*, Zorannes suffered the loss of a father who was murdered by a king, and of his be-trothed, Orbella, once his mistress, who marries the murderer.

Such parallels are inconclusive evidence. But the seventeenth century provides another clue concerning Ophelia. Jeremy Collier in his *Short View* observed with reference to her that if Shakespeare was "resolved to drown the lady like a kitten, he should have set her a-swimming a little sooner. To keep her alive only to sully her reputation and discover the rankness of her breath was very cruel." In the next century, Voltaire unhesitatingly called her Hamlet's mistress.[3] In 1829, the German critic Boerne sug-gested that she had been seduced by Hamlet.[4] And in our own day, Allar-dyce Nicholl in *Studies in Shakespeare* raises what John Draper calls "the old question of her chastity with Hamlet."[5] In 1951, E. G. Clark of Hunter College, in an educational broadcast over the Fordham University radio station interpreted Shakespeare's play in the light of Ophelia's Valentine song and propounded the view that Ophelia was pregnant. Thus there is an old and persistent tradition which questions Ophelia's virtue. The tradition antedates Shakespeare, is influential in his own play, and is still current.

Another significant instance of the erotic estimate is to be found in *Der Bestrafte Brudermord,* a much controverted play on the Hamlet theme. It may be a redaction of the Kydian drama or of one of the Shakespearean versions. In any case, it parallels the known dramatic versions of the Ham-let story and seems to have been acted in the seventeenth and eighteenth centuries or perhaps earlier. In it Ophelia is a crude, comic character. She

2 Lewis chapter IX.
3 Variorum *Hamlet* (Philadelphia, 1877), II, 381.
4 Ibid., II, 290.
5 pp. 54 ff. John W. Draper, *The Hamlet of Shakespeare's Audience* (Durham, N. C., 1938), p. 55.

complains that Hamlet plagues her, leaving her no peace. The comic element consists in her persistent efforts to induce the effeminate Phantasmo (Osric) to marry her. Ophelia seems to pursue him not because of his virility—which is conspicuously absent—but in an effort to obtain a legal father for her unborn child. She finally corners him and invites him to have dinner alone with her. Unable to escape, he reluctantly assents. "Ah! how merry we shall be!" she cries. With reference to her condition, he sarcastically comments, "It will be right merry,—three eating out of one dish."[6]

Here then is the problem: the sentimental and erotic estimates are both old and plausible. Did Shakespeare intend spectators to regard Ophelia as virtuous or as unchaste?

Though a conclusive answer cannot be given, a solution has already been suggested: Shakespeare intended to arouse uncertainty in his audience concerning Ophelia. Indeed, the creation of uncertainty is dramatically potent throughout the play. *The Tragedy of Hamlet* is a compact of uncertainties, conflicting possibilities, and unsettled problems. What was the true nature of the ghost—illusion, devil damned, honest ghost returned whence no traveler returns, angelic spirit, or antic spook? As Dover Wilson has shown, the evocation of the audience's doubts about the ghost is dramatically functional, is consistent with Hamlet's doubts, and was probably intended by Shakespeare. Other instances of uncertainties may be multiplied. Why did Hamlet delay? Did he delay? Was Gertrude aware of the murder? Had she been Claudius's mistress? Was the pirate attack planned by Hamlet? Did he really love Ophelia? Was Polonius a fool or a capable minister of state or both? Did Fortinbras arrive as a result of some previous arrangement? Was Ophelia innocent or sophisticated or both? Was she chaste or Hamlet's mistress?

Lack of evidence for settling these problems forces resort to conjecture and surmise just as in real life men are inevitably beset with uncertainties concerning most of their fellows. If the play is presented in its own complexities as Shakespeare wrote it, an audience inevitably becomes puzzled by apparent or real inconsistencies and possibilities.

In such uncertainty, in the entertaining of opposing probabilities, in the dialectic of alternatives lies part of the greatness of *Hamlet*. One neglected strand in Shakespeare's rich pattern, the traditional erotic estimate of Ophelia and the persistent linking of her with the idea of unchastity has been restated in this essay, not in order to lessen the dramatic appeal of Ophelia but as a means of emphasizing the strength and stimulus of

6 Variorum *Hamlet*, II, 136 (Act III, sc. xi).

Shakespeare's artistry and as a means of drawing attention to Ophelia's interestingly complex characterization. The consideration of the problem leads to a fuller understanding of the play's richness and other merits and the playwright's techniques and intention.

Something of the essence of the pleasure derived from drama rests in the possibility of many explanations where the author commits himself to none. The possibility of many answers or combinations of them to the problems of interpreting Ophelia adds to her dramatic effectiveness and delightfulness and gives her what Alfred Harbage called "the stimulant effect of non-homogeneous characters in Shakespeare."[7] In the case of Ophelia, Shakespeare did not commit himself finally to any one interpretation; rather, he intended her to remain a problem; he deliberately left her open to a variety of inconsistent interpretations; her interest and part of her significance lie in her non-homogeneity. The possibility that she may have been Hamlet's mistress, that she may have been pregnant, is merely a neglected strand in what might be called her dialectic of opposites.

In real life, completely consistent persons—if they exist—seem unreal; they become "human," alive, convincing, and interesting when inconsistencies are revealed. Similarly, to make characters on the stage seem real, Shakespeare suggests incompatibilities in them; he leaves problems unsettled; he indicates alternatives without clearly deciding between them. Admittedly an audience lacks time for much speculation, but it can be made aware of unsettled problems about a character. A paradox follows: that some element of inconsistency and contradiction often makes a character more credible, real-seeming, and thus more dramatically effective than complete consistency would. The non-homogeneity which Harbage noted in Shakespeare's imaginatively conceived men and women is one of the means whereby they are made to seem flesh and blood, genuine human beings instead of mere actors in a play. Living human beings are interesting when uncertainties, contradictions, and non-homogenous elements are found in them. The same is true of drama. One charm of Ophelia lies in seeing her as she is now conventionally interpreted; another lies in seeing the play and Hamlet and the suicide and his delay in the light of the possibility that Ophelia was his mistress and perhaps pregnant. But the richest charm resides in entertaining both these possibilities, in fluctuating between them, in savoring the complexity and stimulus of the problem of Ophelia.

QUEENS COLLEGE IN THE CITY OF NEW YORK

---

7 Alfred Harbage, *As They Liked It* (New York, 1947), p. 71.

Constituent Elements in Shakespeare's English History Plays

By JOSEPHINE A. PEARCE

I IN THIS PAPER I propose to consider two questions: what constituent elements may be discerned in this group of plays and how have these elements been utilized by Shakespeare in his dramatization of English history? Or we might enquire, in other words, what resources of both substance and of form presented themselves for dramatic handling and, further, with what attitude toward the union of historical fact with poetic drama have these resources been so utilized. This attitude surely marks an advance in creative thinking, for while the extraordinary Tudor interest in the reading and the writing of history was shared by most classes and gave rise to literature in other poetic forms, the English history play appears as a *genre* decidedly new in the latter decades of the sixteenth-century. ,

Historical theory and composition in Tudor times was in the main conservative and derivative, patterning itself on the demonstration of those attributes of history long ago described by Cicero in the balanced phrases doubtless known to every Elizabethan schoolboy. This interpretation of history as the teacher of life invited the historian to organize and interpret the true events of the recent past for the dual purposes of providing political, moral, and religious instruction and of glorifying human endeavor for a world of men who are both moved and judged by God. But during the sixteenth and early seventeenth centuries, as evidenced by the concerns of such historians as Concio, Machiavelli, Raleigh, and Bacon, this traditional theory of the function of history had been re-examined so as to permit the more critical analysis of human causes to modify the older idea of providential causation. Thus, historians sought to be cognizant of the pragmatic value of the interpretation of human behavior, on the one hand, without neglecting the larger interpretation of the working out of God's plan, on the other. It was during this period of re-examination of the theory of history that Shakespeare wrote his English history plays.

We are all familiar with the great repositories of English history provided in their native language by industrious chroniclers and their assistants throughout the Tudor period, and we know that it was from these frequently reprinted tomes that Shakespeare, as well as other historical poets, drew the substance of his factual materials. Two competently written works, Stowe's expansion (1586-7) of Holinshed's *Chronicles of England, Scotland, and Ireland* and Halle's *The Union of the Two Noble and Illustre Families of Lancaster and York* (1548), were Shakespeare's principal sources of English history. Herein he found ample materials for drama—recorded exploits and intrigues of kings and nobles; descriptions of the topography, climate, and beauty of England; and assessments of the character and physical conditions of her peoples. Especially attractive from a dramatist's point of view were what Greene called "the awful lessons of history," the civil conflicts raised and resolved in the course of certain reigns. And especially significant was the controlling idea imposed on the body of historical data, the traditional control afforded by the moral interpretation of events. That Elizabethan dramatists exploited their national history is attested to by the estimate of some two hundred plays dealing with English history and biography enacted in the fifteen year span between the time of the Armanda and the death of Elizabeth. But exactly how faithful to historical fact were these dramatic exploitations of history? What degree of historicity obtains in these plays?

As far as a statement of the distinction between poetry and historiography is concerned, Sidney's placement of the two activities with respect to truth is representative of Elizabethan thought on this matter. Poetry, he writes, "dealeth with universal consideration, . . . and history . . . [with] the particular." But what of the poetic dramatist in relation to history? What liberties did the Elizabethan playwright feel justified in taking with historical fact? That he might supply speeches consistent with the law of inner probability is a 'liberty' imposed on him by the very nature of dramatic composition. That he would ask the audience to adjust its intake of the logically unified procession of event of some years to the output of three hours' traffic on the stage is again a necessity and convention of the medium, consonant even with the practices of the Greeks. There is one liberty the Elizabethan poet and dramatist felt justified in taking with historical event. It is a liberty extensively engaged in by Shakespeare and other playwrights, but I know of only one instance in which it is voiced by a dramatist.

In 1607 Thomas Dekker's play entitled *The Whore of Babylon* was published in London. It was a play dealing with the treasonous threats against the power of Queen Elizabeth offered by the agents of Rome. Dekker prefaced the 1607 publication with a *Lectori,* the first portion of which reads very much like Spenser's Letter to Raleigh that introduces the intention and scope of *The Faerie Queene.* Later on in this *Lectori,* Dekker defends his working method:

> And whereas I may, (by some more curious in
> censure, then sound in judgement) be Critically
> taxed, that I falsifie the account of time, and
> set not down Occurrents, according to their true
> succession, let such (that are so nice of stomach)
> know, that I write as a Poet, not as an Historian,
> and that these two doe not live under one law.

We notice, then, a statement of the liberty which a dramatist felt justified
in taking with historical fact. He feels free to alter not events, but the succession of "Occurrents," or the chronology of events. We notice, further,
that any doubt as to the historicity of the events represented dramatically
is not here anticipated, nor, presumably, considered likely. And certainly
the events of Elizabeth's reign with which Dekker deals in *The Whore of
Babylon* would be well within the memory of his audience, so too the
reports and interpretations of these events, not in chronicles but in contemporary pamphlets and controversial tracts.[1] May we not, then, conclude
that the Elizabethan audience expected a high degree of historical accuracy
from their playwrights and that the playwrights were conscious of this
expectation? Let us now consider how this liberty with the chronology
of events in history operates dramatically and with respect to truth.

Instances of Shakespeare's free manipulation of chronology have been
quite thoroughly noted by scholars, particularly with reference to his
English history plays, and this manipulation has rightly been weighed as
a dramatic expedient. What, for example, except dramatic effect is gained
in *1 Henry IV* by altering Hotspur's age so that he and Prince Hal match
each other's youth? To what other purpose is the king misrepresented as
an old man? And what else actuated Shakespeare's historically premature
reconciliation of Prince Hal and his father? Turning to a few other instances of Shakespeare's manipulation of chronology in his history plays,
we find in *1 Henry VI* a very bold alteration of time in the massing together
of many events which historically took place at times wide apart. Joan of
Arc is represented as the agent by which Rouen is regained by the French,
whereas actually the city was regained long after her death. In this play,
brave Talbot, the terror of the French, is pictured as dying before Joan's
death, but in point of time he outlived her. Again illustrative of this massing of events are such compressions in *King John* as the close concentration
of Papal interference and the placement of the deaths of Queens Elinor
and Constance within three days, instead of three years, of each other.
Richard II, Henry V, Richard III, Henry VIII all likewise reveal the dra-

---

1 I am indebted to Miss Lillian Ardizoni's as yet unpublished study of *The Whore of
Babylon* for the above illustration.

matist pursuing the thread of historic incident in non-historical order. To
be sure, Shakespeare herewith gains a dramatic concentration quite impossible without such manipulation of the time factor. But it would be hard
to maintain that this dramatic concentration, which has been achieved at
the price of historical exactitude, is harmonious with historical truth unless
we can bring ourselves back to Sidney's, Dekker's, and evidently, Shakespeare's concept of the relative freedom enjoyed by the poet as distinguished from the exactitude required of the historian. Both deal with truth.
But the truth a poet seeks is of a higher nature. It resides in the working
out of inescapable consequences of human action, or the working out of
God's plan. And the Elizabethans believed that the power of this kind of
truth remains intact in the shaping hands of a poet and undamaged by his
rearrangement of sequential events. Shakespeare seems to express the
wide latitude of operation bestowed on the poet by the nature of his art.
One of his puppet-poets, a sycophant in *Timon of Athens,* describes this
latitude:

> I have, in this rough work, shaped out a man,
> Whom this beneath world doth embrace and hug
> With amplest entertainment: my free drift
> Halts not particularly, but moves itself
> In a wide sea of wax: no levell'd malice
> Infects one comma in the course I hold,
> But flies an eagle flight, bold and forth on,
> Leaving no tract behind.
>
> *(Timons of Athens,* I.i.43-50)

We have so far observed one of the material resources that presented
themselves to Shakespeare in his dramatization of English history—namely,
the English prose chronicles; and we have further noticed something of
the attitude toward the union of historical fact with poetic drama that he
brought to the handling of his materials, for we have discovered his controlling moral purpose and his sense of freedom in ordering events. We
may now ask what other elements enter into his history plays, and how
do they support or augment the source of historical interest.

One of three enlarging elements, one which bears close connection with
the kernel of historical interest, is the element of political concern. In
the Elizabethan period, political concern could not, perforce, manifest
itself in prolonged and oscillating campaigns nor in legislated programs
for the establishment of political morality, but it showed itself in the
examination of past political lessons for the purpose of understanding and
assessing the political events of the then present. According to current
belief, human nature is unchanging, and history repeats itself. Consequently,

these lessons of the past, already resident in the Chronicles and systematized in the Homilies, could be held up to view so that in them, in their images, the beholder might see the form and figure, the "state and condition of all realmes at all times." And this is what history in a poetic medium, the *Mirror for Magistrates* and its subsequent imitations, earnestly purposed by focussing on individual careers and by penetrating through event to the meaning of event. This kind of work was highly selective, for it chose to represent as its various images only those careers and problems of the past which would best mirror or apply to contemporary situations and, significantly, reflect the accepted political philosophy of the Tudors. Indeed, that Shakespeare's history plays are dramatic mirrors of Elizabethan polity is the thesis of a recent work in the field which contends that in Shakespeare's history plays Elizabethan audiences found images of specific contemporary political situations and conduct.[2] Such an explication of the present in terms of the past forms, however, only a part of the mirror tradition which aspired to make generalizations for "all realmes at all times." The mirror tradition may be found to augment the historical element in Shakespeare's chronicle plays by reinforcing their controlling idea, their moral purpose. This controlling idea illuminates all of Shakespeare's histories considered both individually and as a sequence of plays. Each play mirrors "a local habitation and a name" for a specific political problem: *King John* and the problem of church versus state authority; *Richard II* and the problem of deposition; the Henry IV plays and the problem of rebellion, to name only three. Considered as a sequence, the plays seem to reflect a more than additive image, and of more than mere nationalistic concern is the emergent concept of responsible kingship, of the morality demanded by public office, and of an harmonious body politic.[3]

We considered, earlier, some instances of Shakespeare's free handling of time and the resultant dramatic concentration. Let us now entertain a pertinent corollary to that operation of time change. While the manipulation of the precise order of historical events can produce dramatic effect without the violation of higher truth, it can also contrive new inter-relation of events or orientation of fact without violence to that truth. An example may serve to illustrate this inference. In *Richard II* Shakespeare shows us the usurper Bolingbroke after the murder of King Richard vowing to make a pilgrimage to the Holy Land in order to placate God and expiate his guilt. Holinshed records Henry IV's proposal of the pilgrimage in the last year of his life and without reference to the death of Richard II. Shake-

2 Lily B. Campbell, *Shakespeare's "Histories," Mirrors of Elizabethan Polity* (Huntington Library, 1947), *passim*.
3 Miss Una Ellis-Fermor directs our attention to a larger philosophical unity resident in the work of Shakespeare's Elizabethan and Jacobean phases in *The Frontiers of Drama* (London, 1945), Ch. 3.

speare clearly places two 'events' in a new order and, here, in a new significant relationship. In succeeding plays the reproach of defective sovereignty runs steadily through the usurper's career; indeed, in the crisis of the war with France his son prays God to discount his inherited defect. Shakespeare, then, in *Richard II* contrives two facts into a new relationship. The point is that it is a moral relationship, and its amplifications assist in giving meaning to the plays. It would seem that the dramatist felt justified not only in altering the chronology of historical events for the purpose of dramatic intensification, but also in bringing historical events into new relationships in order to mirror more cogently the moral interpretation of political life.

We have already anticipated the function of an element which enters into Shakespeare's art, the element of construction. For we have seen that in order to make his mirror of truth brighter he has re-assembled certain of his materials in such a way that they more clearly image the moral interpretation of history. To enquire into construction is to enquire into the connection between matter and idea, or to enquire into the assemblage and organization of matter (dramatically, incident) with relation to idea and purpose. That is, *construction* exactly in the sense employed by a builder—whether he be an architect of integrity or a fly-by-night contractor—to indicate the structural relationship between the building materials and the building itself. The most recent study of the function of construction in Shakespeare,[4] indeed the only responsible and illuminating study I know of this neglected aspect of Shakespeare's art, discovers to us just how the dramatist's controlling idea in a given play determines the structure of that play and at the same time how the structure of the play bodies forth and secures the controlling idea. Matter and idea are not dissociate; they are fused by the binding energy of construction.

The multiple facets of Shakespeare's original and powerful constructive art cannot here be our proper concern, but we are obliged in our consideration of the history plays to recognize that Shakespeare's controlling idea in one play is not manifested in one combatant character, one partisan point of view, one locale. The concept of the proper areas of church and state authority in *King John,* for example, is not mirrored forth by either the King or the Papal Emissary, nor by the commodity of the defecting English nobles, nor does it find expression in England rather than in France. Shakespeare mirrors his controlling idea in a prismatic fashion, by breaking it up into the interactions of many characters and situations, and sometimes, as in this play, by collecting it in a character or little

4 H. T. Price, "Construction in Shakespeare," *University of Michigan Contributions in Modern Philology,* No. 17, May, 1951.

scene outside the press of action. These rapidly shifting interactions block out or determine the logical construction of the play in the larger sense.

A smaller aspect of construction, that of the intimate relationship between matter and style, between the idea or emotion to be expressed and the form of its expression, brings us to a third great reservoir whose resources Shakespeare utilized in the history plays. The first two resources, Tudor histories and the Mirror tradition, offer him substance and purpose; the third, rhetoric, offers him not thematic materials but modal design in support of his construction. Rhetoric may be described as that patterning of language by which action or idea is given a surcharge of stimulation. It is not fundamentally responsible for fixing on the particular action or idea to be expressed, but for the manner in which that action or idea takes on form.

In accordance with the doctrine of literary imitation, early Elizabethan writers of both prose and poetry utilized the formal nature of classical rhetoric, thereby approximating themselves more closely to the courtly intelligentsia. And the formal rhetoric of the ancient world operative as a shaping influence on early Elizabethan drama of a serious nature is that of Seneca. Shakespeare's early work, particularly the history plays, reveals an extensive reliance on formal or stylized rhetoric as a means of surcharging his dramatic event or moment, of crystallizing out character, and of unifying his construction. The whole question of the influence, either direct or indirect, of Seneca on the early Shakespeare is still under consideration by scholars, and there seem to be generally pervasive convictions about significant parallels in philosophic content, situations, and characters. As if Shakespeare got blood and ghosts from Seneca; he got them from bodies. The ghost in *Richard III* is Clarence's not Seneca's. Surely a man is entitled to his own! Those scholars who find a Senecan influence on Shakespeare operating in construction, however, are in a better position to interpret these parallels to us. They can tell us more accurately that the resemblances between Seneca and Shakespeare lie in matters of structure, in formal rhetorical patterns, and in rhetorical irony, rather than in matters of dramatic materials.

The Renaissance classification of rhetorical figures astonishes a modern not only by reason of the intricate names of its categories, but also by the fact of its complexity and inclusiveness. Illustrations of Shakespeare's use of formal rhetoric (both *genus* and *species*) are readily available in various scholarly studies,[5] and the observation that Shakespeare in his development as a dramatist effects an emancipation from formalism in style and thought

---

5 Sister Miriam Joseph, C.S.C., *Shakespeare's Use of the Arts of Language* (Columbia University Press, 1947) should be noted especially.

has been made.[6] We can see Shakespeare advancing toward this emancipation even within the series of his history plays.

Historical materials, moral purpose, organic structure, and some stylized rhetoric—these do not alone constitute the substance and the form of Shakespeare's history plays. We have yet to ask ourselves, I think, at least one more kind of question: how did Falstaff get in? of what account is a lesson in English? what place have leeks in history? We have already observed something of the freedom that Shakespeare exercises as a dramatist of history; here, again, is another augmenting element. It is the same kind of freedom that is apparent in the native romantic drama of Elizabethan England, which is, in general, without any perfectly fixed dramatic technique or any singular dramatic tone. The native romantic trend in drama encouraged Shakespeare in his operational freedom, for it presented no formalized critical dicta that would restrain him, no Aristotle. Like the native romantic drama, certain of Shakespeare's histories make no strict division between tragedy and comedy, and as natural as the play of children are the movements from the serious to the comic in these plays. This freedom of movement represents a way of telling a story; it is not symptomatic of the nature of that story. The Henry IV and Henry V plays embrace comic materials not because it was thought that life in England during those reigns was any happier, nor because audiences of 1598-1600 were more dedicated to levity than were those of a few years before, but because Shakespeare's conception of the components and structure of drama is undergoing change in the direction of that poise and mastery of both matter and form which characterizes creative genius.

At this point our minds return to Shakespeare's image which twins his own creative experience and suggests to us the range and plasticity of the medium in which he operates:

> my free drift
> Halts not particularly, but moves itself
> In a wide sea of wax.

UNIVERSITY OF MISSOURI

---

6 Hardin Craig, "The Shackling of Accidents: A Study of Elizabethan Tragedy," *PQ*, XIX (1940), 1-19.